NEXT LEVEL YOU

How I transformed my life with mindfulness and meditation

By Oksana Esberard

SattvaMe

www.sattva.me

CONTENTS

FOREWORD

by Andy Bailey

Remember the last time you stood on the edge of a lake, on top of a ridge, or were up early enough to see the sunrise? Remember that singular moment when you were still enough to feel the simplicity, beauty, and expansiveness of those sights? That moment, that feeling is how I now describe mindfulness to other hyperachieving entrepreneurs and leaders of business.

I met Oksana Esberard during one of the most stress-filled times of my life. I had been building my third business for about 6 years at that point with much success and massive amounts of effort. I had sacrificed much for this success, still do today, but I was missing something. I have always been a very fast mover. Quick decisions, relentless execution, and "no try" attitude were my pillars getting me where I wanted to go. And still, something was missing.

That something turned out to be mindfulness. I

had heard the term for years, always equating it to meditation, and never felt that it was something that I should do, nor that I had the time for it. But turns out it is much more than just meditation. In its purest form, for me, it is gaining the ability through practice to be present in the moment. Just like in those moments of inspiration I now seek out in nature, mindfulness practice under the leadership of Oksana has given me new insights into myself and has helped me find what has been missing. Myself.

If you, like me, are someone that feels like there is more to this whole thing than just achieving; or, like me, feels you need to learn how to slow down your thoughts so you can respond rather than react to every situation; or, like me, feels stuck and are looking for more from your life; then making mindfulness and its practice part of your life may be a solution. It was for me.

Oksana's latest book, NEXT LEVEL YOU, weaves the powerful story of "why" she has the insight and ability to assist entrepreneurs and leaders like me—and maybe you—to discover more for yourself.

INTRODUCTION

I have worked with hundreds of successful entrepreneurs and executives. No matter how accomplished, they are still in search of something grander, something they cannot buy or achieve. Nearly none of them experience a true sense of fulfillment, happiness, unity, and peace regularly. Most people suffer from a busy negative mind, spend little-to-no time taking regular breaks, and use caffeine and alcohol to recharge. Sadly, even in our advanced times, we still do not enjoy life at its full potential.

Stress has become a valid source of energy, excitement, and inspiration. And stress is also debilitating. Seeing the effects stress can have on us truly pains me. *Not enough time? Having a hard time sleeping? Wish you had better relationships with yourself and others? Feeling tired and overwhelmed more often than not?*

Experiencing the negative impact of stress firsthand, I have seen how stress and anxiety have ruled the majority of my life. And I have seen countless examples of busy professionals being overwhelmed and burned out under the pressures of a fast-paced reality. They are still struggling to stop, stretching themselves too far.

Today, the outdated trend of overachieving at all costs is losing its relevance, but there are no models to replace it. We still aspire to be successful, but we see success and stress as a one-package deal.

Is there another way?

Success without stress is possible! My own personal transformation from stressed to balanced, while still being successful, inspired me to write this book and reflect back on the tools I used to make this transformation.

By embracing the practices of mindfulness and meditation, I have changed my life. I am a different, better person. I am more successful, more fulfilled, more joyful, and more purpose driven than I ever could have imagined.

This book is a vulnerable attempt to share stories, from my Soviet Union upbringing to becoming a citizen of the world and an impactful entrepreneur, energizing leaders to be agents of change and to win. All of this is possible because I embraced mindfulness and meditation practices.

Important to note that in this book, I am not supporting any religious associations or belief systems. Instead, I use my story and incorporate scientific research to demonstrate how mindfulness and meditation can help you find balance in your life. Please note that nothing in this book replaces any medical advice from your healthcare physician.

NEXT LEVEL YOU is a combination of personal stories, practices, and research designed to educate, inspire, and energize you to jump-start or deepen your meditation and mindfulness practice. I hope it helps you navigate this turbulent, information-overloaded world and transform your life from busy and stressed to balanced and energized.

I am passionate about mindfulness and meditation because I have seen countless transformations in others, and I am inspired to energize more change. These tools will help you reach the next level in whatever drives you—becoming a better leader, a better professional, a better human being.

Welcome to the NEXT LEVEL YOU!

Mindfully,

Oksana Esberard

DEDICATION

To the humankind. May we expand to our highest human potential.

ACKNOWLEDGEMENTS

Many wonderful beings have helped me bring this book to life.

Thank you to my teachers Anand Mehrotra and Tommy Rosen and all the master teachers in the Sattva Community. You gave me the wisdom, tools, and hope that I could transform my life, even when I could not see it myself.

I have deep gratitude for my parents, Vyacheslav and Irina Klimovich, who put their lives at risk to provide me with the education and opportunities that I would not have otherwise.

Grand "Thank You" to Rafael Esberard, who has been a source of strength and inspiration for many of my endeavors. This book is another example of friendship, love, and support, which I am grateful for in my life.

Big thank you to my host-family Barry Huggins and Janet Kennedy, who helped me fulfill my "American Dream." And thank you to Karen and Glen Hill, who welcomed me as their daughter all these years.

A special thank you to Andy Bailey, who inspired and held me accountable for writing this book and building SattvaMe into a sustainable business. Andy, sorry for making fun of your office the first time we talked. Now my office looks like yours, and I am proud of it every single day.

Thank you to my students and clients, who gave me their trust and embraced the tools of mindfulness and meditation to improve their lives and careers. A special thank you to Krista Wade, Doug Skoke, Stephanie Cruz, Kaity Ersek, and Ryan Markel for sharing their stories and successes.

Thank you for all the hard work and dedication to my editors, Kaity Ersek and Eva Greenholt. You girls put up with much more than you signed up for, and I am grateful for your friendship.

Thank you to my friends and family for the suggestions, revisions, and dealing with my countless doubts and insecurities: Rafael Esberard, Lauren Rangel, Barry Huggins, and Karen Hill.

Thank you to Andy Buyting, Jessica Embree, and Erika MacLeod with Tulip Media Group for making the publishing process so seamless and enjoyable. Without your guidance, I would be lost in the marketing trenches.

Thank you to the Petra Coach team for helping me brainstorm the title and tagline, especially Jennifer Faught, Chip Gallent, JT Terrell, and Ryan Markel.

Thank you to LBMG Marketing, the Laurens, for continuous support with this book and SattvaMe.

A special place in my heart goes to Lola, my amazing dog-friend, who has been my "stress barometer" and unconditional supporter at all times.

And thank you to all the readers for your curiosity and willingness to reach the NEXT LEVEL YOU with mindfulness and meditation.

CHAPTER 1
FAR, FAR AWAY

"The greater the awareness - the greater the capacity."
- Anand Mehrotra

One warm Floridian evening, I was running back from Fort Lauderdale Beach where I go to meditate sometimes. It was around 8 pm and it was dark. I was listening to a podcast as my body moved at a steady pace. As I ran, I noticed a few couples holding hands. I felt love, peace, and unity in the air magnified by the incredible weather and the ocean breeze.

When I started running along one of the bridges that connect the beach to the main city, I noticed headphones, sneakers, a cell phone and keys scattered on the ground. I looked up and there was a young, slender woman on the rail of the bridge, ready to jump. I stopped in my tracks and immediately grabbed her by the hand.

"What are you doing, beautiful?" I asked her. She was shaking uncontrollably and tears were running down her face.

"Nobody cares," she uttered, sobbing with pain in her voice and face.

"Why don't you come down from the rail so we

can talk?" I pleaded without letting go of her hand. She refused and continued to cry. I held on to her.

I asked her a few basic questions to understand if anything tragic had happened with her family, personal life, or at work. She replied "No" to everything. She also denied being under any influence of drugs or alcohol. She seemed sober to me.

I can't remember exactly what I was telling her. I just kept talking, trying to find something that would resonate with her and make her laugh. Eventually, she started to open up to a conversation.

She told me she was 25 years old, and that she lived and worked in the area. Nothing specific from her life put up a red flag. She seemed to have a normal life. She had a family with siblings, cousins, and nephews. Her parents were alive and well. She had a job and was not in any harmful relationships. On the surface, everything seemed fine. But she confessed that she had been feeling extreme loneliness and sadness for a few years now.

> "Nobody gives a damn about me. The world is such a dark place," she kept repeating.
> "That's not true," I said softly. "I care. Why would I be here with you if I didn't?"

That visibly puzzled her, and she started to pay more attention to my words.

> "How do you know everyone is living a perfect life except for you?" I inquired.
> "Instagram."

I had read about this misconception with millennials and younger generations, but here in front of me was living proof. This young woman was suffering from unfair comparisons and perfections that social media creates in an untrained mind. All the rising suicide rate statistics flashed in my memory. Chills went up to my spine from seeing it in action.

I asked her again to come off the rail, but she refused. Then I pretended I would climb up to her so we could talk, which made her come down immediately.

She collapsed on the ground, her body still shaking from crying so hard. She was shattered, mentally and emotionally. At the same moment, a car stopped, and the driver inside the vehicle asked if we needed help. I didn't know what to say. I had never been in a situation like this. In my head, I wished for the police to arrive. I didn't dare say it out loud because I was afraid of scaring her. Instead, I just shrugged my shoulders and drew my attention back to the young lady. The driver left.

The young woman in front of me was expressing so much emotional pain, confusion, and hopelessness. According to her, she felt miserable while everyone else was living a happy life. Her family, her friends, her coworkers didn't care about her. She felt insignificant and small in a big, cold world.

To my surprise, in some ways, she resembled me eight years prior on the 51st floor on the balcony of my luxury condo. I felt like I was reliving my own pain and confusion, only this time I had the answer, especially when she asked hopelessly:

"What's the point of life?"

"The point of life is to evolve," I answered with confidence. "So you can experience more joy despite the pain that is inevitable. Look around you. What do you see?"

"Darkness and people walking by without caring," she stated with a sad, blunt look on her face.

"Well, I see a beautiful Floridian night, filled with stars, a magical breeze, and water. I see couples holding hands with love. I feel unity and joy. Am I not in the exact same place with you at the same time right now?"

"Yes."

"Then how come we see such different things?" I continued. "Could it be that it is the state of our consciousness that determines our experiences in life?"

She looked deep into my eyes, listening with her whole being.

"You are feeling sad and lonely, as I once felt. And your experience of the world reflects that. I am here to tell you that there is another point of view. You can see the same world differently if you choose to change the story you have been telling yourself. Yes, there is pain and aloneness in the world, but there is so much beauty and connection too. Open yourself up to joy. It is here, and we all long to experience it."

The comparison between me of eight years ago and me of now was stark. By hearing myself speaking to this young woman, I saw how much I had expanded in my inner capacity to see the diversity of life. I realized that the world is not sad or happy, good or bad. The world just is. The universe simply exists regardless of what we think about it. It existed before humanity and will continue after we are gone. How we experience life in the moment is up to us.

The way we perceive everything is based on the mental and emotional states we are in. Gaining the capacity to choose states that support joy, peace, happiness, understanding, connection, and fulfillment on demand is the essence of self-mastery. Most of the time, we are so stressed and busy that we mindlessly react to our external environment instead of taking the time to find awareness and respond from a calm, creative, balanced state of mind.

The only way out of the reaction loop is to evolve our thoughts, feelings, and actions. Evolution is the primary purpose of life. We are here on Earth not to earn money or get married. We are here to become better people every day. When we get stuck or choose to stay in our comfort zone, life gets worse with time. That's the law of nature that we can verify with our own experience. As a result of staying mediocre, we get absorbed by pain that is an inevitable part of human existence or we stumble upon joy and get trapped trying to replicate it.

By training our mind and emotional resilience, we create the capacity to transcend emotional and physical pain and perceive the beauty of the world, both in joy and sadness. We get to choose our world, by releasing the negative tendencies of the mind and correcting the limiting conditioning on an emotional level. That's how one can lose a loved one and remain grateful. Or be in prison for several decades and come out as a stronger person than before.

Limiting conditioning means that love and happiness have to look a certain way. We learn that if you have this type of body, then you are worthy. If you are in a relationship, then you have love. If you buy things, then you have happiness. External validation drives our inner states. As a result, we learn to dumb down the profound expansive states that we once felt as kids. We forget the times when things did not matter, and the inner world was more real, infinite, and meaningful.

Our expressions of happiness, love, joy, and creativity cannot be confined to a particular "look and feel." We are all different, and each of us uniquely experiences life. Confinement to unrealistic parameters leads to confusion, separation, competition, and loneliness, which is then magnified by the internet and the insecurities it creates.

I told this young lady my brief story and how daily meditation and mindfulness practices helped me. I painted a picture of my current life. She was listening intently and stopped sobbing. We even laughed a few times, and I saw the life starting to shine in her eyes. I offered her a hug.

At that moment, a police car pulled over. Two officers came out of the car and proceeded to ask her questions. She started to cry again and admitted that she intended to commit suicide. While about to be handcuffed, the sobbing girl asked if she could get the hug I had offered earlier. I hugged her warmly and assured her that everything would be alright, that she would now get help.

While one officer was assisting her to the police car, the other thanked me for staying with her. He explained that they received a call about an attempted suicide about a half-hour ago, but no officers could get here right away. He asked for my statement and contact information.

I asked him if I should leave my contact information for the young lady, but he advised against it. "You never know what the story is with them. She will go through a round of testing and will get therapy," he assured me.

I made it back home, profoundly impacted by the experience. I told the story to my husband. Emotions caught up with me from revisiting my past self through this young woman. I felt her pain, I knew her world way too well. And I was grateful that I had created a different reality for myself.

* * *

My story begins like the opening scene of any Star Wars movie: *A long time ago in a galaxy far, far away.* I grew up in the USSR, a country that no longer exists, in a town called Dalnegorsk, which translates to "Far Mountains" in English.

How remote was it? Imagine a map of Russia. Now trace your finger along it to the far east, further than Siberia. You will find yourself at the Russian Pacific coast, which lies between China and the northern islands of Japan. The closest city you may have heard of is Vladivostok, one of the major seaports in the area. Now go north into the mountains—13 hours by bus or eight hours by car along the east coast. That's the spot.

When I explain to people where I come from, I like to add "Think of nowhere in Russia . . . go a bit further. Got it? Now find the spot in the middle of this nowhere. This is where I am from." The chances of finding something grand in life from Dalnegorsk are slim to none.

My parents, originally from Siberia, were sent to Dalnegorsk by the USSR government, along with a group of geologists, right after they graduated from university. Their job was to develop Dalnegorsk's then-emerging mining operation. To ensure that the government kept them together, and likewise, moved them together, they married while at university. It wasn't long after arriving at Dalnegorsk that they had my sister, eight years my senior, and my brother, six years my senior, which makes me the baby in the family. We had no immediate relatives in the town, nor did they ever visit. Dalnegorsk was simply too far, even by Russian standards.

As a child, I felt like I had won the lottery growing up in this faraway land. The area was picturesque with nature all around. There was a sense of complete freedom, discovery, self-expression, and adventure. We grew our own food and always had farm animals and pets as companions.

I would swim in the rivers, lakes, and sea, and go fishing and camping with my family. During the summer, we would spend three weeks at a time on the wild seashore, living in tents, cooking on an open fire, and bathing in freshwater streams. We would catch or harvest our own "meal of the day" which was often fish and wild mushrooms. I would spend hours in awe staring up at the diamond-like stars in the night sky and at the gold of the crackling fire.

Then summers would switch to colorful falls and snowy winters. For a child, there are no limits to imagination and creativity when faced with a pile of snow. You could be and do anything, making castles and empires, and dreaming of courageous victories with princesses and dragons. It was better than *Game of Thrones*; it was real and mine.

Nature was my first unconscious experience with mindfulness and meditation. There I found a dynamic silence emerging as an unspoken realization of the grandiosity of everything in this universe and beyond. This silence makes everything clearer, more inclusive, and full of possibilities.

To me, it is the meaning of life itself. The blend of fulfillment and joy that represents all plains of human existence: physical, mental, emotional, and spiritual. Extreme sports adventurists, artists, and psychologists also call it a *flow state*. Words cannot describe the impact of this all-encompassing feeling. You can only experience it, and once you do, you want more and more of it.

As a kid, words like mindfulness and meditation were not part of my vocabulary, but I lived by the principles. I found nature so captivating that I would sit in silence and observe, listen, and merge with it for hours on end. Sometimes I would close my eyes and disappear into the nothingness and timelessness of nature. I was complete. I was enough. Little did I know, I was in deep meditation.

Most people think of Russia's Asian region as rural and remote. In reality, it is very similar to the remote areas of Montana, Wyoming, or other northwestern states in the United States and western Canada. The difference between remote areas and cities is in the profound peace and connection with nature. In my far, far away town, I felt complete and whole.

It is interesting that my childhood connection with nature rings true in today's scientific research, describing how nature impacts our ability for deep focus, self-awareness, and happiness. Nature does not have any judgments or opinions, likes or dislikes. It exists in silence and peace. Therefore, it is easy for the scattered mind to rebuild a connection with nature, which creates a profound healing effect on our body and mind.

I did not know that by digging potatoes with my bare hands and bare feet that I was "earthing and grounding." Scientists have tested how the connection to the ground stimulates healing effects within our body and mind.

Research on earthing or grounding presents simple and accessible health strategies against chronic inflammation, stress, and excess of toxins, which is the leading cause of major modern diseases such as cardiovascular disease, cancer, and all sorts of mental illnesses, from Alzheimer's to depression.

To put it simply, the earth is full of free electrons that bind with positively charged free radicals (or toxins) through the skin. It neutralizes inflammation fast and it is drug-free. According to researchers James L. Oschman, Gaétan Chevalier, and Richard Brown, "[g]rounding appears to improve sleep, normalize the day-night cortisol rhythm, reduce pain, reduce stress, shift the autonomic nervous system from sympathetic toward parasympathetic activation, increase heart rate variability, speed wound healing, and reduce blood viscosity."

After reading this research, I realized why, as a kid, I have no memories of depression, chronic pain, or fatigue. Any scratches and wounds (and I had plenty from all the climbing and exploring) would heal quickly like the tail on a lizard. Once I moved to the big city, a simple bruise would stay for weeks and months at a time. That is because "grounding reduces or even prevents the cardinal signs of inflammation following injury: redness, heat, swelling, pain, and loss of function." The lack of connection with the earth leaves mild inflammation and pain untreated.

All you need to take advantage of this "technology" is to walk barefoot or make direct contact with the ground through your feet, hands and other body parts. Not so easily done in the modern world of big, concrete-developed cities. Most of us work and live above ground in tall office buildings and condominiums. The higher the floor, the more prestigious and expensive real estate gets. What a paradox!

For those who live in cities and want to heal through nature, there are now grounding mats, mattresses, sheets, and earthing bands to connect your shoes and wrists. Or, you can always opt for the old-fashioned way and go for a walk in the park and sit on the ground during a lunch break or phone meeting.

As wonderful as my early childhood was, the Soviet Union projected gross limitations on the physiological and psychological elements of my upbringing. Electricity and warmth were scarce, even during the winter.
Loss of electricity created food shortages.

As the youngest in the family, with few responsibilities, I was in charge of getting our bread. Fresh bread was a luxury, and to get some, I would stand in line for four to five hours. Since it was common to buy six to eight loaves at a time, if you were at the end of the line, frequently the baker would run out before your turn.

Once the USSR collapsed in 1991, the peoples' lives only grew worse. Both of my parents, as did many others in town, lost their stable jobs and had to get creative to survive. Without any business education, my parents converted to self-made entrepreneurs, stretching their physical, mental, and emotional boundaries. They would go to China to buy clothing, carry it literally on their backs through the Chinese-Russian border, and then resell it to people living in remote mountain areas.

The toll on our family was huge. During my parents' trips to China, I would stay alone for weeks at a time, as early as age 10. Friends and teachers never noticed. I would take care of pets and farm animals as well as keep up with school. Pairing these responsibilities with teenage struggles of self-worth and a lack of belonging to my original peer group, it is easy to see how nature remained my only refuge until I left my "far, far away" town.

My first break into the big, unknown world was at the age of 16. As an excellent student who was passionate about English, I won a yearlong scholarship from the American government to live and study in the United States. The program was called FLEX (Future Leaders Exchange) and it paid all of my expenses. A family from Arlington, Texas, volunteered to host me.

My FLEX exchange year altered the trajectory of my life. Coming from chauvinistic Russia and Soviet "sameness," the United States was the first time I saw opportunities for a different, grander life. My 16-year-old self lit up with a desire to build my future outside of my homeland, possibly in America.

Unfortunately, there was a gross limitation to making my dreams possible. My visa mandated that I had to go back to Russia for at least two years before returning. After seeking legal advice, I found that nothing could be done to change this mandate. My heart broke and my mind rebelled, but there was no solution other than to comply. When my exchange year was over, I moved to Moscow, where my parents had relocated while I was abroad.

At 17, I lost my place in the world. I quickly found that I did not belong in the big city. Moscow felt like a giant meat grinder. People seemed more robotic, rushing from one thing to the next, without emotion, without vitality. Aggression and anger were the most dominant human expressions. Everyone seemed doomed and fighting for limited (in their minds) resources. But going back to my "far, far away" was not an option either. The area was economically devastated and slowly dying. It had no opportunities, nor future.

There are no mountains in Moscow, and finding a natural oasis is rare. Just like in any big city, parks and other natural habitats are filled with people, noises, and modern conveniences, such as restaurants, stalls, and concert stages. The sky is gloomy, with short spurts of sun and daylight. Moscow feels physically heavier, but the mental and emotional toll it takes on people makes it feel even worse.

I suddenly found myself in an adult world where the value of money and material possessions was at its peak. In my hometown, we relied on self-sufficient farming and needed little cash to live a good life. In Moscow, for the first time, I felt "lesser than" because neither I nor my parents had a large bank account, fancy clothing, or a car. Years later, even after traveling to over 55 countries, I still find Moscow to have one of the most superficial cultures concerning financial status.

At the time, I did not understand why I was trying so hard to fit into this superficial society. I wanted to belong, I wanted to matter. Lucky for me, I was tall, young, and pretty, so I was accepted into many circles that I would not have otherwise been allowed.

That is when I joined the modeling industry for a few years. As a result, my ego grew larger. My standards and values dropped to an unimaginable low of trading time and beauty for money. In modeling, I was welcomed not because I was smart and hardworking but because I was pretty and was favored by important, usually much older, men. Typical, high-society Russia.

Later, I learned that this superficial outlook was not just a flaw in Moscow. It is a global human weakness of young women that are eager for luxury and adventure. I saw it in social and business circles in Asia, Latin America, and the United States. In retrospect, for me, Moscow was the perfect training ground to experience the divided world based on egos and power.

> The stronger the ego and the set rules of *right and wrong*, the further we get from the natural happiness and wholeness of self. Instead, the present moment loses out to the never-ending race to achieve and have more. The ego justifies it with the societal rules of survival and success.
>
> We start saying things like "*But I have to work to pay my bills*" without realizing when enough is enough. Money, status, and prestige trump well-being, happiness, and contentment.

My ego grew larger when I was accepted to the best university in Russia. Now, I wanted more and more material goods at any cost. Unfortunately, the principles of well-being and humbleness were not something that I was taught by the university nor by the adults in my life.

I lived a double life. Secretly, I was longing to go back to nature and drop all this "theater of appearances." I deeply disliked where I was and who I was becoming in comparison to the happy Dalnegorsk girl who still lived inside me. At the same time, I was playing along with the environment I was in, becoming more egoistic, money-oriented, arrogant, and close-hearted.

Strangely enough, I now see that the disconnect between inner visions and outer manifested reality is where the majority of people get stuck. It feels like a waiting room. You know you do not belong where you are, but you find yourself powerless to change anything.

So you choose to wait for a wave to carry you out to some new grounds.

That wave may never come. It is up to us to rescue ourselves from the waiting room or to stay there and decorate it with all the "stuff" we get as compensation.

With my vision of the United States in my mind, I did not want to wait. Together with my host family, we desperately tried to garner my return to the United States, but I was denied a visa twice. I spoke with politicians and academics, meanwhile earning a degree in Business Management and a second degree in English translation just to keep my language skills fresh.

At last, four years later, an opportunity presented itself. I received an invitation and scholarship for a business program affiliated with FLEX at Lehigh University in Pennsylvania. I knew that this would be my chance to fulfill a burning desire to live in America. At 21 years old, I got a visa and came to the United States with just two suitcases.

I was happy to start a new life! If only someone had told me what it takes to be an immigrant in a foreign country—I might have chosen to stay in Moscow . . .

CHAPTER 2

THE AMERICAN DREAM

"Whenever you see a successful person, you only see the
public glories, never the private sacrifices to reach them."
- Vaibhav Shah

The flight from Moscow to New York felt heavy. I had been so obsessed with making my dream of returning to the United States come true, that when it was time to prepare to leave, I operated on autopilot. I remember little from that period. I mindlessly organized, packed, and strategized, without considering what I was giving up by leaving Russia.

On the plane ride over, everything seemed to catch up to me. Even though I did not like my life in Russia, it had become familiar, and it was a product of my own making. Over the past four years, I had put so much work into making Moscow feel like my home. I was in my junior year at a prestigious university, my family and friends were in Moscow, everything I knew about myself—the good and the bad—were connected to Russia. Going to the United States meant leaving everything behind and stepping into the unknown with no guarantee of success.

It was during this time that I started to consider what

makes many people stay in familiar jobs, relationships, and cities. What is their driving reason for sameness even though deep inside they are longing for something grander, for new possibilities?

My answer . . .Stability. We can either be in a growth or stability mind-set. Most people are searching for ways to feel safe and secure, and many of us mistake being stuck with stability. But, the nature of life is to change, not stagnate. Unless we evolve, things get worse with time. And eventually, the desire for growth knocks on our door as a sense of dissatisfaction, no matter how much stability we attain.

I had watched the lives of my family, friends, and neighbors and had compared them to the lives of the Americans I had met during my exchange year. I knew that staying in Russia would not give me what I wanted for my life. That perspective of long-term vision made the short-term losses of leaving Russia worth it. To me, leaving was the only choice, at least so I thought.

I was lucky to discover early on that there was a stark difference between the economic development of Russia and the United States. From that point, I knew that staying in my comfort zone was not a solution for me. Moving was a "choiceless" choice—I wanted growth.

But what happens when the leap from good to great is not that obvious, like in developed countries? We stagnate. We accumulate. We protect and build walls of security. We freeze from an inability to let go of what is already in our hands to reach out for something different and grander in the future. We get stuck because we know that growth comes with a cost.

The hardest part of making the move across continents was experiencing my new life all by myself without the guidance of my friends and family in Russia. Instead of receiving their expected support, they were mad at me for leaving. They openly told me that I was abandoning and betraying them by moving. When my dad, the one who I adored and thought to be the most reasonable and compassionate amongst my family, said he felt the same as the others, I was crushed.

When I first moved, I tried to replace my emotional roots with Russia with a connection to the members of the Russian-speaking community. But they did not give me the support I needed.

Instead of being more empathetic with another Russian-speaking immigrant that was struggling with making a big move, they were far from compassionate. Moreover, they were extremely competitive.

> Behavioral science backs this trend. According to a *Harvard Business Review* article entitled "It's Harder to Empathize with People If You've Been in Their Shoes" by Rachel Rutan, Mary-Hunter McDonnell, and Loran Nordgren, there is an "empathy gap" when looking for compassion from people that have similarly struggled. Instead, they tend to be biased because their own success gives them the right to expect that others "stick it out."

> According to the researchers, teachers that
> have been bullied are often less compassionate
> to students that have been bullied. Individuals
> that have struggled with unemployment are less
> compassionate to others in unemployment.

Even though I did not receive a warm, empathetic welcome from the Russians that were already rooted in the United States, to my surprise, Americans could not empathize with me either. Without being in my shoes, they could not relate to my pain and acknowledge my emotional sadness. When I talked about my struggles, Americans would point out that great things were ahead of me as a way to cheer me up, which did not help. For nonimmigrants, I was a brave, intelligent young woman charging for her American Dream. Whereas, I was actually anxious and looking for stability and affirmation that everything would be okay from someone who had already found their American Dream.

After spending the first three months at Lehigh University, I transferred my student visa to Texas Woman's University in Denton, Texas. The contrast of Denton to chic Moscow and my egoistic standards was painful. People were nice and helpful, but I was closed off. This was not the university of my choice but a necessity to maintain my student visa and legal status. My ego was telling me that I should be somewhere grander. My thoughts were focused only on getting out of Texas. I knew I would have to move soon, so why bother connecting? By the middle of the fall semester, I was already planning my next move.

During my first year in the United States, I felt lonely and misplaced. Without knowing how to deal with these emotions, I poured myself into my studies and work. To make up for the lack of emotional security, I was doing double the effort compared to other students and colleagues, only to exhaust myself physically and mentally. It worked in the moment because my workload distracted me from my emotional pain. But it backfired later.

Around Thanksgiving break, I visited Miami. It was love at first sight. The exotic palm trees and beaches were an exact contrast to gloomy Russia and the space of the Lone Star State. I loved the abundance of parties and the Latin community presence. I also wanted to pursue a degree in hospitality, and Miami was home to Florida International University—one of the best hospitality schools in the nation. By Christmas, I waved good-bye to everyone I knew in Texas, without much explanation.

At last, I felt like I had found a way to replace my connection with nature. It was in Miami where I regained the ability to dissolve into nothingness and to be free, open, and joyful again. But instead of being in nature as I did when I was a kid in the far-far mountains of Russia, I was finding solace in the house music and drinks of Miami's nightclubs and endless parties.

The world would disappear. My body would feel free in the movement of dance. My mind and emotions, uplifted from alcohol and smoking, made me feel "high" on life again! Until I woke up the next day...

The morning after a party was always horrible. The "higher" I would get at night, the "lower" I would drop in the morning. The hangovers, dehydration, headaches, irritation, and negativity made me barely functional at work and school. It was too high a price to pay for the inner freedom that I was attempting to replicate. But I did not know about any other alternatives; it worked and I craved it.

I was slowly suiciding, while maintaining an illusion of a happy life.

As humans, we often stick to short-term fixes even if it hurts us in the long run. Stanford's "Marshmallow Experiment" is an innocent illustration of how this phenomenon of instant gratification impacts our life-long desire for more. In the study, kids decide whether to have one marshmallow (or cookie or pretzel) now or to wait ten minutes and receive two rewards instead. More often than not, kids would choose the initial marshmallow rather than wait ten minutes to receive two.

As adults, we are still too scared to let go of what is in front of us, like a drink or a TV channel that brings immediate relief. The promise of something grander, like a good night's sleep, is too far into the future.

We keep the jobs we do not like because we crave safety and control. We take painkillers to numb the pain when we want to be healthy again, without assessing the cause of the pain. Ultimately, we value the illusion of health and stability and avoid doing what it takes to be truly healthy and financially free.

In fact, our craving for immediate solutions gets our society into major trouble. We postpone true happiness, health, and freedom until the inner conflict explodes and we can't take it. As a result, we burn out, get horribly sick, and commit suicide in large numbers.

No wonder rates for "death of despair"—which include suicides, liver sclerosis, and overdose—have been rising for the past 15 years. To be clear, abuse of alcohol and opioid-related deaths are considered slow suicides in the medical community. As stated by *Science Daily*, "... absolute decline in life expectancy [in the USA] relative to other countries and in various measures of psychosocial well-being have been observed starting as early as 1980."

Being in a relationship to ultimately form a family was high on my priorities. It is a huge part of societal expectations in Russia, and a source of pressure on women.

From my state of despair, I looked for the right partner. And, where would I find him? In a nightclub, of course.

But I did not want just any guy. I was on a quest to meet the Prince Charming who would make life easier for me. I was stuck in the fairy tales that I read as a kid. As a result, I was hanging out with a lot of assholes.

My disconnection with what really mattered in life hurt my ability to choose a partner wisely. Instead, I was searching for a partner based on his looks (he had to be tall!), what car he drove, if he paid on our dates, where he lived, and whether he had a high-status job or entrepreneurial career.

My partner also had to be smart and a world traveler. His behavior was secondary. At the time, I believed that I was so special that, when he fell in love with me, he would treat me like a princess, regardless of how he treated others. Often, young men would not meet the "financial" cut. Most of the men I was attracted to were over 40 (already a red flag to them for being in a nightclub).

Most men I met were not interested in having a family. They were obnoxious, narcissistic, selfish, and only interested in validating their ego through sex with pretty young women. And they used their money and empty promises to reach their goal. I fell into their trap over and over again, which made me even more hurt and lonely.

Finally, my desperation pushed me into a relationship for the sake of being in one. Despite all odds, I met a really nice guy. But he did not fit into my "Prince Charming" ideal. He was not my type of handsome: he was a young immigrant with little financial stability and no lucrative job. It was a quick fix to my loneliness, which he filled like a band-aid on a broken leg.

Despite being in a relationship, nothing changed my mental and emotional well-being. I continued to find my sense of unity in nightclubs because my boyfriend was working in the industry and could get me to even bigger, better VIP parties and events. I was living a lie, a happiness that was not sustainable. Until I woke up one day and realized that I was with the wrong person, doing wrong things, and surrounded by meaningless things.

I came to this realization sitting at home on the balcony of a beautiful condo on the 51st floor of a luxury Miami high-rise, overlooking Biscayne Bay and the Atlantic Ocean. I had just received a green card, confirming that I was a resident of the United States. It was a huge accomplishment for any immigrant. My boyfriend was ready to marry me. I had a great job, paying me more than I could ever hope for at my age. I drove a brand-new car and even had a dog.

And yet, despite attaining my American Dream, I felt depressed and anxious, asking myself *Is there more to life?* Not knowing the answers, I became overwhelmed with fear and despair, realizing that this was not the life I desired nor wanted to continue. It was one of the darkest moments in my life. A huge wake-up call, which I was not eager to receive.

Up until this moment, I lived by the concept of "When... then...". I put all the power on the external conditions around me to become happy. I would say things like, *When I get a green card, a promotion, a boyfriend, a dog, a car . . . then I'd really be happy.* The paradox is that all these things were happening for me, but the happiness that arrived was short-lived. It would last a few weeks, sometimes a few months. But then I would need to raise the bar and create another condition to strive for the happiness to return.

Deep inside I knew there had to be another source of happiness and contentment.

Since childhood, I have had an incredible curiosity about the essence of life. I would often ask myself questions like *Who am I?, Why am I here?, What is the purpose of my life?, and How can I be happy?*

But, like most of us, I had no idea how to look inside myself for the answers. Nor did I get answers from school and adults. Everyone was pointing somewhere outside: study hard, work hard, and happiness will arrive. Now with perspective, I am able to see that it did not work for those people either.

I did what I was told, with all my heart and soul. I moved from my home country and left the people I loved only to realize that while education, money, and stuff may play a role in life, something big was missing. I felt this missing element as I sat in my posh Miami apartment, with tears running down my face, despite the fact that I was living a life that many would consider a success. My heart was aching. My soul was empty. I felt like a failure, and I did not want to live in such a dark world.

Without knowing how to deal with the anxiety and fear (or any emotional imbalance that I was now frequently experiencing), I acted like a cornered animal in fight-or-flight mode who only wanted to escape. I reasoned that if I could not fix the situation, it would be best to leave it all behind and start over.

One of the ways that I found strength for this next move was by blaming the US immigration system that took so much time and money. I blamed my boyfriend for being too nice and not being the "Prince Charming" I wanted. I blamed my employer and even my dog. It worked and gave me the push I needed. In a few short weeks, I packed my bags and arrived at the furthest place I could find from Miami—Hong Kong.

I started a new chapter in life and titled it "Searching" because that was what I was doing. Per visa requirements, I had to leave Hong Kong every two weeks to be able to stay for two more. During this period, I traveled around Asia and the world extensively and absurdly. In reality, I was running from my desperate self.

As you can imagine, moving to another part of the world did not fix anything. After about six months, once the thrill of being somewhere new wore off, I found myself wondering again about the meaning of life. *What am I doing here? Could the circumstances possibly get any worse?*

And then it got so much worse...

CHAPTER 3

BECOMING AWARE

"Whenever you find yourself on the side of the majority, it is time to pause and reflect." - Mark Twain

Five months after I arrived in Hong Kong, I found myself in a 60-square-foot apartment. It was the smallest apartment I had ever been in. It was so tiny that when I extended my arms on both sides and tried to rotate my body, I could touch either the kitchen cabinets or the wall next to the mattress. The bathroom was even smaller. To sit on the toilet, I had to push my hips to the back of the seat and rest my knees against the cabinet in front of me.

One morning, sitting in my tiny apartment, the phone rang. It was my mom. She never called me; I usually called her. I answered the phone, and in a grave tone, she explained that my dad was in a critical condition in the hospital. A gas lamp had exploded in his hands, causing him to fall off the roof of a newly built garage. Not only did he break his spine, shoulder, and multiple small bones, but most of his body was covered in third-degree burns.

Within 24 hours, I was in Moscow with my family.

The next ten days dragged on in agony, the unknown looming in front of us. During this period, I met with my dad once. It was the last time we spoke and saw each other. On the 10th day, my dad died at the age of 62.

My father's death became an unimaginable rock bottom. We had a connection beyond words, which was my secret weapon in life. I did not get a chance to tell him, but my dad gave me the strength to move to the United States by myself at a young age. His presence fueled my inspiration to study with honors while building a new life in a foreign country, because of the hope that one day we could all live together happily in America. I persevered through challenges that otherwise would make no sense to endure. I always kept in mind that if something went terribly wrong, I could go back to my family in Russia. And now my life was half empty and filled with pain.

I found myself completely numb, capable of only crying, followed by restless sleep. All I could think about was that he was gone, leaving a grander void in an already weakened heart.

I traveled to Alaska and Latin America to distract from the loss. Eventually, I returned to my tiny apartment in Hong Kong. My moods often switched between severe anxiety and deep depression. I felt more fear and uncertainty than in Miami. There were days when I could not sit still, while other days I was so depressed that I could not lift myself off the pillow after 18 hours of sleep.

Suicide crossed my mind often.

Despite reaching this low point, I found a new experience of mindfulness. Mindfulness, as defined by John Kabat-Zinn, who is the first to bring it to medical and scientific research, is the ability to cultivate and sustain "awareness that arises through paying attention, on purpose, in the present moment, nonjudgmentally . . . in the service of self-understanding and wisdom."

Most can achieve a state of mindfulness while being outdoors. In nature, all of our senses activate at once so we become present and aware. Nature does not have judgments and opinions, which creates an experience of unity that manifests in the body as feelings of joy and awe. When we disconnect from the chatter in our mind and connect to nature, we enter a state of flow, self-reflection, and contemplation, which are the prerequisites for self-understanding and personal development.

I experienced a completely different take on mindfulness when I went clubbing. The music was so loud that I could not hear my own thoughts. My senses would be dulled from drinking and smoking, so my body would experience joy while being fully present in the music and the movement of the dance. This type of mindfulness comes at a cost of detoxification the next day. Otherwise, if you have ever been to a club sober, you know how disturbing and loud it actually feels.

When we experience extreme amounts of mental and emotional pain over a prolonged period of time, we can also become mindful because the pain anchors us to the present moment. However, "extreme" and "prolonged" are the keywords. When you have severe, short-term physical pain, that is all you can pay attention to and the state of mindfulness does not occur. The mind becomes very loud. It judges and complains, making you feel miserable.

The intensity and the length of the pain eventually shut the mind off, resulting in a state of mindfulness. That is why many people report profound transformations while being in accidents or after overcoming extreme hardships.

That is the state of mindfulness and flow that I started to experience. After exhausting myself from grief, I would become present and aware of the emptiness inside my body and mind. I would drop into a dark void behind my closed eyes. It felt soothing and calm there. By activating the inner wisdom of silence and stillness, my body and mind were triggering the innate ability to recover from trauma.

Now, with the science of mindfulness and meditation, we can activate the innate wisdom for mental and emotional transformation on demand, without going through the hardships. That is why these tools have gained so much popularity—they make sense!

The prerequisite for mindfulness is the ability to be present. The present moment is the only time when we are in charge of our thoughts, emotions, and actions and have the capacity to change them at will. Becoming aware of the present is the skill that separates humans from the rest of the animal kingdom. It enables us to become the creator of our own life experiences, living more in the flow and less in confusion.

Unfortunately, because of socioeconomic conditioning and technological advances, we have moved away from our innate natural flow, and ultimately, we have lost the skill of being present. Today we need tools like mindfulness and meditation in our daily life to maintain the equilibrium of presence among busyness. Otherwise, we suffer.

In my darkest moments, when my mind could not fight or escape the death of my father, I would come to a full acceptance of reality. I had no strength to wish that things were different. I could not run away from myself anymore. Grief became the time to reevaluate my life and face my inner struggles.

As a strong, uncompromising overachiever, it was hard to accept that I was stuck and could not escape reality. But with time, I recognized that I could no longer rely on myself to crawl out of my depression. I needed help.

After a few months, a friend recommended a place called the Shakti Healing Circle based in Central Hong Kong. Run by a husband-and-wife team, this wellness center specialized in energy healing, meditation, yoga, and other alternative healing practices. I signed up for private coaching on grief with the husband, Stephen, and energy healing with his wife, Pervin.

Through deep reflection, it became clear that my move from Miami was a reaction to my mental and emotional burnout and an attempt to escape from my core issues. I had blamed others and my surroundings to avoid taking personal responsibility for my mess.

I was determined to change my life for the better.

During the next few months, I became certified in Transcendental Meditation and completed two levels in Reiki energy healing techniques, which originated in Japan. I hired a nutritionist who made profound changes to my diet. I began to practice yoga 3–4 times a week to balance the intensity of my body and mind.

By adding new holistic practices to my daily routine, I started to rise from the emotional pain, confusion, and anxiety that had ruled my life. It was not an overnight fix, but a humble start that, little by little, was changing the trajectory of my life for the better.

> Human nature is such that we are more likely to make permanent changes towards balance only when we reach a level of dissatisfaction with life below our tolerance. We all experience ups and downs, but there are some events—like death, divorce, and disease—that make us say *No more, I don't want to continue to feel, think, and live this way.* Usually, it is this deep state of desperation that provokes us to face the challenge of changing ourselves instead of changing everything around us.

Tony Robbins said, "Change happens when the pain of staying the same is greater than the pain of changing." I believe that we can also change when the innate desire to evolve and reach the next level is greater than our satisfaction with our comfort zone. We do not always need to rely on pain to grow. I wish I had made this discovery sooner.

Finding Shakti Healing Circle after my father's death gave me the gift of seeing the difference between an energy-deprived and an energy- rich life. I call it a gift because I could have found refuge in drugs, alcohol, and who knows what else to cope with my loss. In fact, I was already relying on alcohol, travel, and partying to numb the dissatisfaction and anxiety that made me move from Miami in the first place. Before my dad's accident, I was living an energy-less life without knowing it.

The energy-less state manifests in mindlessly doing what needs to be done in life, whether it is education, home, and work affairs or managing social appearances.

Average human existence revolves around maintaining the state of "okay-ness," where things do not feel great but also not terribly wrong. It almost feels like we are half-asleep and half-awake, switching on autopilot in the morning and turning it off at night.

Life goes in motion. All seems fine, except for the unsettling feeling deep inside. The feeling that we may be robbed of time and the capacity to do something grander, something that we truly love and enjoy. Things like hobbies, exercising, being in nature, or spending more time with the people we love. We stop doing what feels good and makes us happier by justifying it with work and family responsibilities, career ambitions, and the necessities to meet the expectations of others. We are afraid we would be judged if we start doing what we love and not what has to be done.

In the energy-less life, we are not provoked to have deep thoughts about why we do what we do or what we would choose to do if there were no bills to pay. *No time. No energy. You can't have it all. I will do it when...* is the narrative that follows.

To keep us in the state of "okay-ness," we are trained to look for quick fixes: tired—drink coffee; sick—take a pill. Marketing gimmicks promise to solve the issues that we create in the first place. Doctors and pharmaceutical companies guarantee to fix ever-increasing health problems. But keep going, do not stop to think and contemplate.

Whereas, all it takes is to realize that we have the power to change by pausing and finding the solution that lies within us.

The alternative to an energy-less state is the energy-rich life that I glimpsed into when working with Pervin and Stephen. An energy-rich life is where we operate from the state of flow, balance, and contentment. It is a life where we do what we love, and it energizes us to do more and be better for ourselves, for others, and for the whole world. It is a life where we are intimidated by the challenges and excited to take them on because we love who we are, what we do, and are thrilled to share it with others.

The paradox is that an energy-rich life requires less effort than an energy-less existence, and it gives a larger return in terms of stability, fulfillment, and happiness.

Why don't people choose to live an energy-rich life then? Because there is a cost to switching that most are not equipped to pay. I call it the hangover of changing the habit. Mindfulness and meditation with proper guidance provide powerful solutions to combat the hangover of change. But, in the beginning, it requires commitment and effort.

A journey to an energy-rich life is challenging because it involves gradual change. The modern, fast-paced world does not praise anything gradual. We want it yesterday. Nor are our brains wired to favor change as shown by recent neuroscience.

> It is fascinating that only 1 out of 10 people will change their lifestyle when told that they will die within a couple of months if they do not make the change!

To find and sustain the balance between energy-less and energy-rich states, we must look at life as a finite experiment where the result is the legacy we leave after our death. Keeping the end (death) in mind puts a sense of urgency on the things that matter most and allows us to ignore the small stuff. It inspires us to view events differently than if we were immortal. Mindfulness, or living in the present moment, adds richness to savoring and treasuring all of life—good, bad, and otherwise.

Holistic resources, such as mindfulness and meditation, make permanent changes to our energy levels because they act as strong reminders on what is important, not what grabs our attention. Mindfulness and meditation offer an opening for people who consider themselves well but unconsciously engage in escapism through workaholism, social outings, alcohol, and other substances and activities that do not result in leaving a legacy for future generations. An energy-rich life is not something you achieve once and it stays forever. It requires practice to access self-mastery. It calls for consistency to explore and overcome painful human experiences. And it is sustained through accountability to test that you have become who you aspire to be.

The good news is that we have a built-in capacity to change. To activate an energy-rich life, you need self-awareness, patience, trust, curiosity, and a set of new skills that mindfulness and meditation enable us to develop. All are accessible in the silence and stillness of the practice.

Notes:

_____

_____

_____

_____

_____

_____

_____

_____

_____

_____

_____

_____

_____

_____

_____

_____

_____

_____

CHAPTER 4

THE POWER OF STILLNESS

"All men's miseries derive from not being able to sit in a quiet room alone." - Blaise Pascal

During my first visit to Shakti Healing Circle, I was full of grief from the loss of my dad and the psychological pain from the restlessness I had been experiencing ever since I left Russia. All I wanted was to feel good again. Yet, in my mind, I could hear the negative self-talk: *Why are you here? Who are these people? How could you fall so low?*

My logical mind could easily accept Stephen as a guide. Stephen was British, and he came to the wellness field after a corporate career.

Our first session together was groundbreaking.

Stephen: "Tell me about your dad."

Silence. A massive ball of tension was lodged in my heart and throat, blocking my ability to speak. A waterfall of tears was falling down my face.

I finally uttered: "I miss him so much."

Through the tears, I told Stephen about all of the broken plans. My dad would never see my wedding. His grandkids would never meet him. There was no more time to spend together in perfect silence.

Stephen: "Why don't you talk to him about that? Your dad is part of you. Even though he is not physically present, you can still have a conversation with him. Do you want to try?"
I silently agreed.

Stephen walked me through a guided meditation, where I visualized my dad and me together. At first, there were tears and hugs, then we talked. The experience made me feel like a huge weight was lifted from my heart.

The impact of the exercise excited me. Up until that moment, I had been treating my dad as nonexistent, where in reality, he was fully alive within me. I could still talk to him. I could write him a letter. I could revisit the places we had been together.

At last, I had found a solution to my pain by reconnecting with my dad through meditation. Yet, I never seemed to have time for it. There was always something in the way. It was never the right time, or I did not have enough time, or I was not in the right place. I kept postponing the exercise until Pervin helped me understand what had been stopping me.

Pervin and Stephen were very different. Pervin was from India and more mystical. She had a quality of groundedness and poise that I had never seen before.

At first, I was not as accepting of her instruction as Stephen's. Unlike Stephen, Pervin would not give me logical explanations nor did she tolerate my inflated ego. My limiting beliefs about Indian culture were blocking my perceptions. Coming from a chauvinistic culture, I also could not accept a woman as a role model.

However, I could not deny how much better her energy healing sessions made me feel. I would immediately notice a positive change in my state of mind and a lightness in my body. This feeling of mental and emotional relief lured me to come back for more.

During one of our sessions, she stopped me, looked me straight in the eyes, and said, "You have a problem with stillness."

She went on by saying that it was *my addiction to action*—constantly doing something for the sake of avoiding stillness—that prevents me from healing. I was confused. Of course, I could sit still, who couldn't?

Noticing my disbelief, Pervin tasked me with an exercise. Each day, at about the same time, I was to sit still in one spot for two minutes without movement (scratching and fidgeting were not allowed). My eyes could be opened or closed, but they could not watch anything in particular. No distractions. Pure stillness.

I thought it would be an easy task, yet within the first 10 to 15 seconds, I felt a strong impulse to get up. I was suddenly thirsty, or I would remember that I had forgotten to turn the lights off, or I needed to check the stove. My mind would get into a panic mode about what I had not done yet. It was both a frustrating and eye-opening experience.

I call it the "watching the corn pop" exercise, as an analogy to microwaving popcorn. Have you ever watched the timer as the popcorn pops? Try it for two minutes, in absolute stillness. Time will barely move. And if your mind is as distracted as mine was, it may drive you crazy.

POPCORN CHALLENGE:

Stop everything you are doing and sit alone for two minutes in stillness and silence without any distractions. No technology, no reading, being in a quiet space indoors or outside.

Reflection:
- What thoughts have you noticed arisen within your mind?
- What emotions have you noticed?
- What were the sensations and impulses within your body?
- What was surprising or curious about this experience?

According to Pervin's explanation, reconnecting with my dad required stillness. But my body and mind were conditioned for constant action as a way to escape from facing my inner struggles.

In today's society, we are wired to constantly be in motion—both physically and mentally. We have lost touch with the value of stillness, deep contemplation, and silence. Instead, we live in times where full calendars, cluttered email inboxes, and busy schedules are associated with efficiency, success, and high performance. We have become addicted to action.

Dr. Gabor Maté, renowned addiction expert, speaker, and author, defines addiction as "any behavior that a person finds pleasure or relief in and craves but suffers negative consequences and cannot give up."

For me, *action addiction* is any behavior that we may or may not be aware of, but we use it as an escape mechanism to avoid being present or confronting issues that create an imbalance in our lives. We continue taking destructive action while maintaining the illusion that we can stop and be present at any time.

Worrying is a widespread example of how action addiction manifests in our life. Worrying solves nothing. It is a destructive illusion of the mind, yet it makes us feel like we are engaging with the problem in a productive way. Not worrying requires conscious awareness and the ability to control thoughts and emotions. Most people are unaware that they are worrying or unable to stop worrying at will.

For example, think back to the last time you sat in traffic, waited in a long line, or ran late to a meeting. At some point, a narrative in your mind appeared with subtle or strong feelings of anxiety, anger, frustration, hopelessness. *Will this ever end? Why does it always happen to me? I am not going to make it...*

Where attention goes, energy flows. Worrying starts to grow like a snowball going down a slope. As the voice and feelings of anxiety magnify, some people cannot contain it within themselves. They start to complain, check their phone, talk to someone, looking for an outlet for their inner disturbance. All of these actions feel like we are doing something to solve the issue, but in reality, we are only adding more stress.

When we allow action addiction to control our lives, physical consequences manifest. Because of the excess stress that we create by letting our mind and emotions run wild, our immune system lowers, and we experience chronic fatigue and pain. To solve these new issues, we consume medications, sugar, caffeine, and alcohol, which overtax our body and nervous system even further. Excess of stimulants results in issues with sleep and generate a lack of rest, which over time manifests as disease.

> Modern society suffers from mental illnesses, burnout, autoimmune disorders, stress, and cancer more than ever before. The National Institutes of Health (NIH) estimates that 23.5 million Americans are diagnosed with autoimmune diseases while nine million Americans are diagnosed with cancer, and 22 million with heart disease. Both the incidence and prevalence of autoimmune diseases have been increasing worldwide.

However, the solution is simple and accessible to everyone. It is stillness, both of the mind and body. In stillness and in silence, we avoid adding unnecessary suffering to an existing life situation and open up the ability to find creative solutions.

Traffic, lines, bad weather, and accidents happen. They are outside our control. However, adding our negative self-talk to life events only makes us feel worse compared to choosing to stay neutral and maintaining inner balance and contentment. You can verify this with your own experience.

Since I have used stillness as my tool, normally frustrating situations clear up faster and with less drama. As my resilience against previously painful life experiences soars, I feel more energy and drive to continue the day in a good mood.

And there are even more benefits to stillness. It also helps us to tap into our intuition, which is otherwise blocked by the noise of our mind.

Imagine having a book with all of life's scenarios written within its pages. It has answers to all of the essential and nonsensical questions you have ever had and could tell you everything about your past, present, and future. Now realize that you already have this book. It is your intuition.

You are the one that holds all of the answers to your questions about life. You are the unique expression of all consciousness around you, known as the unified quantum field, which you access through awareness and intuition.

Today, this consciousness field is widely researched by scientists like Frank Wilczek at MIT and Dr. Daniel Litim at the University of Sussex, among many others. But it is also something that yogis and ancient communities have known for thousands of years.

As an individual expression of all consciousness, you are the only one that ever was, is, and ever will be. You are unique and ever evolving, which means that the choices and actions you make or write in the chapters of your book determine the relevancy of the answers you receive at any point in your life.

Some of these questions could be *Who am I? What is my purpose? What should I do in life?*

You read glimpses of your book unconsciously when you make important decisions.

Consider the last time you analyzed whether you were making a good choice or not. You most likely collected all the facts and information available first. At some point, you looked inside yourself to verify if a decision "felt right." Unconsciously, you know how to check back with yourself to make sure you are making the best choice possible.

Unfortunately, few of us stop to "read" our book and many are not aware that it exists. Just like reading a regular book, reading the book of your life requires stillness. Yet, action addiction makes stillness difficult. We constantly move around either physically or within our minds. We rush, we run, we push. And when we finally sit still, we either pass out from exhaustion or feel anxious to get up again.

Why don't we take the time to stop and read our book when we know that the answers are available to us? There are many valid reasons for this answer. Yet, in short, we are conditioned to take action as a way to reach success, which we generally define as material possessions or status.

Action gives us an illusion of control. Few people relate success as a state of being. But, in reality, we can be imprisoned and still find happiness and fulfillment.

Recently, I discovered a program called Hustle 2.0 that serves incarcerated people. Most of the program's participants spent decades in prison, and some have a lifetime to go. Yet, once they graduate from the program, some participants become more successful than people who have never been arrested. They call themselves "Mavericks," and they create charities, mentorship programs, and support groups despite the physical limitation of being behind bars and having felony records.

For Mavericks, success is first a state of mind, not the ability to take action. At no surprise to me, the Mavericks conduct mental exercises that train stillness and patience like meditation, contemplation, and visualization.

From childhood, we subconsciously learn to hate stillness. As kids, we want to explore the world by being active in it. We run around and touch things. But adults constantly tell us to sit still and not to touch anything.

Consider the school system that requires us to sit still for hours on end. This forced stillness creates a rebel mentality because it is against our innate nature to move and explore. As Neil DeGrasse Tyson, an educator and astrophysicist, put it, "the first few years we are taught to walk and talk, so then the rest of life we are told to shut up and sit."

In our adult life, the pendulum swings the other way. We start to believe that action is the answer to everything. "Taking action" is much sexier than "finding stillness." We learn that constantly doing something makes us feel useful to society. Action, combined with our childhood dislike of stillness, becomes our conditioned identity and the way to live life. But is it the only choice?

I once tasked the "watching the corn pop" exercise to a hyperactive client. First, she listed a thousand reasons why she could not take the time to follow through on the exercise.

She complained that her work made finding time impossible—even though she worked only two days per week. When at home, she claimed her kids and dog took constant time and attention. In reality, she could carve out the time to do the "watching the corn pop" exercise. After all, the exercise takes two minutes out of the 1,440 minutes we get daily. But her subconscious mind resisted the idea of stillness while her consciousness was finding no time for exercise and justifying it with excuses from her daily life.

The interesting part was that she believed she was capable of stopping and taking a break at any moment — *if only she had the time.*

Despite different modalities of action addiction, a distorted relationship with time is a common denominator. People with different levels of addiction feel like they lack time and it results in a desire to take more action.

In this world of overachievement, the action becomes a double-edged sword. When we have some energy to spend, taking the time to stop and reset feels counterintuitive. As a result, we exhaust ourselves in order to give ourselves permission to take a break.

For the sake of our sanity, we must correct our perception of what stillness represents.

Look at the stillness in nature. It is dynamic, graceful, and purposeful. Animals can sunbathe for hours and then suddenly move with extreme speed. Even the largest and the most ferocious predators, like wild cats and crocodiles, spend most of their time in stillness and restful relaxation, preserving their energy and moving with the flow of life. Stillness strikes birds at the peak of their mating dance when they spread their wings to show their best feathers. All animals know when to pause at the right time.

Human bodies also have a built-in, natural technology for performance, rest, and recovery through stillness. When we rest, our body activates recovery mode, managed by the parasympathetic nervous system. Sadly, our modern environment resists this natural mechanism. Then our logical minds justify the urge to recover with the necessity to perform. One more email, one more meeting, one more thing to cross off our endless "to-do" list, until we are energy-less, burnt out, and sick.

To bring back the balance of action and stillness, we must wake up from the trance of action addiction and instead tap into our biological wiring. In fact, we already do it through sleep (or the resemblance of what sleep should be for many of us).

> During sleep, our brain shuts off. We become still and unconscious so our biological body can rejuvenate. And yet, we are not spending enough time snoozing. Today, the average American sleeps just 6.8 hours each night—with 40 percent sleeping less than six hours. In 1910, this average was nine hours, according to *Forbes*.
>
> Research shows that sleep deprivation affects our mind and body in the same way as drinking. We make more mistakes and take a longer time to complete tasks. And it feels nasty too. A study by *The Lancet* revealed how a group of sleep-deprived physicians took 14 percent longer to finish a task and made 20 percent more mistakes compared to peers who were rested.

To take advantage of the benefits of stillness, the easiest thing we can do is improve our relationship with sleep.

It is both the quantity and the quality of rest that impacts energy levels and well-being. Modern lifestyles are destructive to good sleep. Stress, technology, and constant exposure to light all have impacted our ability to rest well. Therefore, we must be intentional and consistent in our striving for a good night's sleep.

10 TIPS FOR BETTER SLEEP:

1. **Think in sleep cycles, not hours:** We sleep in 90-minute sleep cycles, and our body needs at least 4 cycles per night for the full biological reset. That means that we must get a minimum of 6 hours of sleep per night. Getting fewer results in sleep deprivation and loss of performance.

2. **Find out what is your optimal rest time and stick to it:** Most people need 6, 7.5, or 9 hours of sleep. Typical advice for 8 hours a night puts you in the midst of the sleep cycle, and you may feel restless upon awakening.

3. **You snooze—you win:** If you wake up drowsy and tired, chances are your alarm rang in the middle of the sleep cycle. In such cases, give yourself 15–30 minutes more to "finish the dream." With time, you will notice when the sleep cycle ends and you will wake up easier.

4. **Expose yourself to natural light:** 15–20 minutes of sun/daylight in the morning stimulates the production of the sleep hormone melatonin at night.

5. **Pay attention to artificial light:** Exposure to LED and blue light disrupts the secretion of melatonin. Dim all bright lights and avoid technology at least an hour before bedtime. Candles and salt lamps give a perfect light for a relaxing atmosphere.

6. **Resist drinking caffeine after 2 pm:** Caffeine excites our nervous system and stays in our body for 6–8 hours, which may prolong your bedtime.

7. **Avoid alcohol 1–2 hours before bedtime:** Even though you might fall asleep easier, alcohol reduces the overall quality of your sleep due to dehydration and intoxication.

8. **Exercise at least 4–6 hours before bedtime:** Physical activity right before sleep excites the body and mind and you might stay awake for longer than planned.

9. **Have sex before bedtime:** The hormones released during sex promote good sleep.

10. **Meditate:** Follow your breath, use mantra, or do a body scan before or while lying in bed, especially if you have issues with "racing mind."

Bonus Gift: Download free "Restful Sleep" meditation under book section on www.Sattva. Me website.

Stillness during the day is another natural way for our body to activate recovery mode. It improves decision making, focus, creativity, and emotional regulation.

What is the trick? Napping is one option, and it has

become increasingly popular. A second—the one I recommend—is meditation.

In meditation, our body is asleep while our mind is awake. In this state of awareness, the nervous system is in restorative stress-free mode and releases a bouquet of healing hormones. So, meditation is like taking a nap, but with the added benefit of self-awareness and self-correction as we observe the contents of our mind.

Many people feel sleepy when they start meditating. That is because when meditating, our brain waves function similarly to when we fall asleep. In the beginning, the brain cannot tell the difference between falling asleep and meditation, so it slips into our default unconscious state. It gets better with practice as you learn the subtle difference between these states. If you start to meditate and cannot hold your head up—then take a nap instead. Your body knows what it needs, and by becoming still, you allow it to tell you how to rejuvenate in the most efficient way.

Contemplation and reflection are other forms of stillness. Pausing and thinking about our work, life, and relationships is paramount to letting our brain and body sync.

Journaling forces us to slow down and think. It helps us slow our thoughts so we can analyze them and see any patterns that either fill us with energy or cause us stress.

To break the cycle of constant action, we must schedule a time to be still and meditate. Scheduling stillness ensures that we make the time. Stillness is a conscious decision to reconnect with the essence of who we are and regain the ability to discover the answers written within our life book. It is the gift of human awareness, helping us to reach the next level in our mental and emotional evolution.

We are so used to constant motion that for many people, stillness feels uncomfortable, strange, and annoying. It can make us feel anxious and sometimes feels like a waste of time. If that is how you feel—congratulations! All of these feelings mean you are on the right track to breaking your action addiction.

I must admit that there was a time when I was not all that different from my hyperactive client. I, too, was neither comfortable with nor did I want to participate in the two-minute "watching the corn pop" exercise. But it was what I needed to do in order to recognize my action addiction.

At first, I had to force myself to do the exercise by being held accountable by my wellness coach. But, after a few days of practice, I began to relax and enjoy the exercise. I found relief instead of discomfort and anxiety.

To reach the next level, we must recondition our beliefs from associating stillness with weakness, laziness, and under-performance. We must break the misconception that stillness is for couch potatoes and losers, or, as the saying goes, "You snooze, you lose."

Realize that stillness is energy. Stillness is focus. Stillness improves our decision making so we do not proceed with pointless action. In stillness, we strategize and plan how to take the shortest route towards the goal with a minimal use of resources. There are grace and power in stillness, just like in the pause of a tiger before the jump.

A life worth living includes doing nothing so you can observe its magnificence and be open to its mysteries. It goes beyond our beliefs on overachieving and conditioned tendencies to always be doing something. Stillness allows us time to laugh, be present with loved ones, and catch a spontaneous kind action that you would have missed otherwise.

Stillness is the door to the radically alive *Next Level You.* Would you be willing to walk through this door and discover what is on the other side?

CHAPTER 5

RETURN TO FAR, FAR AWAY

"We are always getting to live, but never living." - Ralph Waldo Emerson

A few years had passed, and I returned to Miami. As I was meditating every day, a natural desire arose in me to go deeper in my understanding of the practice and its history. I started to think about a special gift for my 30th birthday. Instead of an ordinary trip or another party, I thought of a wellness retreat with yoga, detox, and possibly full silence.

One day I saw a Facebook post from my friend Claire, who is also a yoga instructor. The picture captivated me. It was of a beautiful bridge strung over a majestic river, with monkeys sitting on it. The colors were vibrant, and it evoked a feeling of serenity.

"Where is that?" I asked my friend.
"India," she replied.
My immediate reaction was "Ghhhh, does it have to be India?"

India was never on my travel list. In fact, I used to say it would be the last country I would ever visit. There was too much discomfort with little infrastructure and too many unpredictable scenarios. I did not fancy the idea of a modest shared accommodation—offered in ashrams and hotels—in a hot and dusty land. Many bad reviews from friends who had visited India proved my point. I knew nothing about the luxurious and comfortable side of it.

Moreover, the idea of more uncertainty was paralyzing. By this time, my husband Rafael and I were eight months into forming a sales consultancy firm together. I launched into this new venture after resigning from a stressful corporate job without giving myself time to recover, rest, and strategize.

The levels of anxiety and stress associated with new work were unbearable. Founding a business is hard. Doing it with your spouse adds another level of complexity, both in work and marriage. Besides, being trained in hospitality, I had to learn about a new (for me) industry—information technology.

While Rafael was an excellent boss and coach, we realized that we needed to separate our business and relationship in order to make both of them work. I was the one to leave, but uncertainty and fear paralyzed me from taking the action. I was desperately in need of peace, stability, and guidance from a new source.

When Claire came back from her trip, there was a different glow to her. She was serene and radiating peace. She told me about the retreat center she visited and the master teacher who founded it. I had a hard time imagining that a place like the one she described existed in India. It had air conditioning, delicious organic food, a spa, and even a swimming pool. Nestled in the lower Himalayas on the bank of a small river, it sounded like heaven on Earth.

The founder and master teacher Anand Mehrotra did not fit into my stereotype of a yogic "guru." He was not an old, long-bearded man in orange robes, as I would imagine an Indian sage. He was a young, modern master yogi. He dressed well, traveled the world, and even drove a Mercedes. My friend was raving about the transformational experience she had, and the glow on her face was even more telling. After watching Anand speak during an online stream, I felt I had found a new guide.

Rafael and I had a long conversation. I needed time to deal with the anxiety of leaving the consulting business and starting a new job. My husband gave me his full support to pursue anything that would help curb my stress and emotional instability. Without looking into other options, I booked a spot for Anand's Sattva Yoga Training.

As a person who likes to have everything in place before committing, I shocked even myself when I booked the trip without having sufficient funds to cover all the expenses related to the retreat. At that point as a family, we had enough money to cover our living costs, but no extra revenue for unexpected trips and training in the Himalayas.

This time, a different flow occurred within me. The

support from my husband and my inner drive to change things for the better removed my hesitation. I knew that if I was meant to be at the retreat, everything would align. It did not make any logical sense, but I trusted my heart.

This newfound sense of trust became a beacon in my future decision making and one of the most profound benefits of mindfulness practice. Because of this trust, I continued to make many "impossible" dreams and experiences come true.

> We think we make the best decisions when we have all the details secure. But how often does that happen? To do the unimaginable, which is the most fun and fulfilling, we need to take a leap of trust. In today's world where all the information is available at the push of a button, trust in the "unknown" becomes a lost skill. The demand for certainty is paralyzing.
>
> Before cell phones and the internet, we would go to restaurants by stumbling upon them, not knowing the reviews. We would take trips to unknown places full of discovery and surprise. We would get lost on a road and be okay asking for directions from strangers. How much more exciting this was!

To ease my anxiety about the trip, I committed to a daily meditation practice with Claire. Once I started to practice the Vedic Himalayan technique she taught me, I felt more at ease and it helped me rediscover this lost art and capacity for spontaneity. She taught me the specific breathwork and a Japa Mala meditation (a meditation technique done with mala beads) that she learned in India.

Almost every morning at 6 am, we met at her beautiful 43rd-floor balcony overlooking the Biscayne Bay and the Miami skyline. It felt like déjà vu from my apartment five years ago. Only instead of being consumed by anxiety and uncertainty, I was stable and grounded through our daily routine and morning tea.

The day of my flight to India, the money dilemma was solved. After a few weeks of negotiations, I accepted a lucrative job offer, so that when I returned home, I would have the funds to pay for the trip. Now I could fully dive into a full month of the unknown in India. It was nerve-racking and I knew my trust would be challenged big time.

When I arrived in New Delhi all my senses were magnified at once. The number of people, cars, colors, spices, and noises were overwhelming. Jet lag helped because I was forced to slow down. Within a 24-hour window, I caught a train to Agra and back to see the Taj Mahal. Once back in New Delhi, I checked into an Indian hotel that I had found on the internet with good reviews and an affordable price.

Quickly, I learned that the reality of India was much different than what Google and the internet told me. There were no similarities whatsoever between what I thought I had booked and where I actually stayed. The 4-star reviewed hotel felt like a 1-star motel in a developing country. Because it was my first time in New Delhi, and I had arrived at 1 am, there was no opportunity for me to look for something better. *Surrender to circumstances* took on a whole new meaning for me that night.

India is like life itself. It gives you at least two choices. You can hate it and complain (but it will not change for you), or you can let go of your preferences and enter its flow. And by entering into the flow, great mysteries unfold. The shady hotel ended up providing me with the best meal and customer service I have experienced in a long time. A five-hour stopover passed seamlessly.

After almost two days since leaving home, I had finally entered the Sattva Yoga Retreat, located in the lower Himalayas, a short flight towards the northeast of New Delhi.

My first training was like nothing I had expected. I thought I was going to India to meditate, be silent, and learn the origin and the history of the yoga postures. Instead, I entered an emotional roller coaster with a full-on transformational experience and release of memories and traumas.

I meditated a lot. But in the beginning, it was not the peaceful, silent experience I imagined. My mind was loud, my body was restless, and my ego struggled with all the self-awareness that came with the practice. Luckily, the retreat was a natural paradise. My worries and frustrations melted away with the lightning speed.

When I arrived at Sattva Yoga Retreat, I was shocked by the similarities to my far-far away home in Russia. I was in remote mountains on a river full of nature, birds, and animals. People were simple and lived by farming and tourism without much development nor a robust city infrastructure.

The place also had the dynamic silence that I had experienced as a child. It felt like nature took me into her arms and gently rocked me to a peaceful state with the lullaby of birds singing. The stress melted away, the rush became irrelevant, and the world was filled with joy. The experience of innocence and raw connection with nature dominated day-to-day existence.

The energy in the Himalayas has a profound grounding impact on everyone, including animals, wild and domestic. These are the happiest stray dogs I had ever seen. Wild monkeys own the towns, flitting from the bridges to roadsides in search of food and items to take from wary travelers. Cows receive respect and food from locals. Everybody and everything coexist seamlessly and with its rhythm.

There is an incredible order to the chaos that rules India. It is a combination that is both enriching yet shocking. I truly believe that you have to come to India at least once to experience the simplicity and abundance of it. In full disclosure, you need a good guide and good recommendations when you go to India. Do not just start exploring the Himalayas on your own or you may find yourself uncomfortable beyond your limits.

The most significant transformation came from the practices I experienced within the Sattva Yoga Retreat. Every day, Master Anand would lead a class, which we called Sattva Journey. He would introduce us to a new sequence of breathwork, meditation, and body movements, sometimes subtle, sometimes full-on physical and large. Sattva Journeys would take us on an emotional roller coaster that were stronger than many other holistic and psychedelic tools I had experienced. As Anand said, it is technology refined by yogis for thousands of years, and it is designed to push us towards self-realization and self-mastery.

During my training, I cried 19 out of 21 days, releasing emotional traumas and memories. Psychologists and pioneers on human conditioning call these memories programming. These are the stories and beliefs usually acquired during our childhood that as adults we put on like a record player and unconsciously follow.

Little did I realize how much mild trauma I had stored inside me over the years. My childhood, teen, and adult struggles were bubbling up from my subconscious memory with events that I thought I had long forgotten.

This subconscious programming is limiting and often redundant, but because we are not aware of it, we do not change the record. The habits, beliefs, and the stories we tell ourselves every day reaffirm our personality and place in the world, diminishing our full potential.

With the practice of yoga and meditation, I started to see some of the programming that my mind held. Many of them were so absurd and irrelevant to my current life that I could change my point of view and behavior immediately. Some programming was complex, with layers of emotional trauma and resistance built upon them.

My conditioning brought me back to grade school. I was verbally bullied from the third grade to my junior year. Despite being rejected by my classmates, I enjoyed studying and did not see why I should make an effort to make friends since I excelled in many classes. I was good at English and math, singing and dancing, playing sports, and doing crafts. Kids were jealous of me and angry that I would not cooperate with them, while teachers would cite me as an example, making the bullying even worse.

As an adult, I created the story that I was not a team player. I hated teamwork and collaboration, which became a huge hindrance in my career. I could not delegate nor take advantage of the group mastermind in anything I did. My relationships were competitive and at times confrontational. I felt like I could not rely on anyone. When I won, I became arrogant and lonely. When I lost, I felt worthless.

During some of the Sattva Journeys, I started to see the story I played in my mind and the origins of it. The tears ran down my cheeks as I realized that as an adult, I do not need to hold on to them anymore. I could be a team player, and I was a good friend to many people all around the world. I was no longer a helpless kid who liked to learn and wanted to do her best. The behavior of isolation and competition that I had adapted in school was no longer relevant.

What is interesting is that my understanding of the importance of teamwork and cooperation did not come from external knowledge like a lecture or a book. The truth came as an inner realization with active visuals in my mind and flashback memories from the past. I started to act differently within the Sattva group right away, by becoming more compassionate and engaged. It was self-realization in action stimulated during long periods of reflective silence and the Himalayan practices called *kriyas*.

Kriya is a combination of movements, sounds, breathing, and inward attention. They are designed and refined by ancient teachers to help practitioners enter into transcendental states by activating the brain, the heart, and energy channels to release and rewire past human conditioning. As a result, we experience richer choices in life with total emotional, physical, mental, and spiritual freedom. As Anand explains, "with consistent practice, where you saw one thing before and would react—instead, you start seeing many options and have the capacity to respond creatively."

Every day there was a new Sattva Journey and new layers of emotions would unfold. In the beginning, my experiences were full of shame, guilt, anger, fear, and lack of self-worth. Then more acceptance, self-love, and joy started to emerge. Sometimes there was so much inner fight that I would scream it out like a lion's roar. We danced and hugged and supported one another as the entire group went through massive transformations. It was the most impactful shared human experience in my life. I was changing inside and out, becoming more alive, clear, and less fearful.

During the day, we gathered for wisdom talks by Anand. He would answer deep questions about Self, relations, and life in such an elegant and simple manner, like no one I heard speak before. *Who are we? Why are we here? What is the purpose of existence? What is the fabric of the universe?*

In Master Anand, I saw and felt what it means to have total self-mastery and unshakable certainty. Before Anand, I had seen it in just a handful of people in the West, and all of them were doing some form of consistent self-practice, usually meditation, breathwork, and yoga.

Anand is spontaneous, energetic, and calm at the same time. There is a radical aliveness to him, which translates to this incredible magnetism that all just want to be around. He speaks from the heart, and it is not to please but to challenge our conditioned ego.

Anand's view of life is so revolutionary and different that there were times when people were triggered and openly disagreed with what he said. We could literally see how the past programming took over the human brain, and the corresponding emotions ran the behavior instead of what felt logical to others in the room.

For example, in India, there is a problem with stray animals. People are accustomed to using stones and sticks to spook them away from their properties. One afternoon, a lady became upset when the retreat guards were using sticks to chase away stray dogs. Later, Anand asked if we wanted to bring up any questions or subjects, and she spoke about her concern for these dogs and the inappropriate (in her view) behavior of the guards.

Instead of making it a respectful inquiry, she started with blame and accusations. It was like a blanket went over her, and she could not remain calm and respectful. She was visibly angry, racist, and confrontational with Anand, while he maintained a calm, unshakable presence.

While observing this woman's reactions, I could see myself back in situations where I had lost my temper and let my emotions run because the reality of life did not match that of another's culture or point of view. This event was the first time, when with full awareness and non judgment, I watched the same anger play on someone else, instead of me, and how emotions can take the best of us.

By observing others, it is easier to notice how our beliefs may blind us to the adversity of life. Without practice, it is incredibly challenging to notice the resistance to other points of view within ourselves, especially when emotionally charged.

Emotional regulation and emotional intelligence are not about knowing that we get angry or overwhelmed. Neither does it mean that we will never experience frustration, sadness, or fear. Emotional regulation is the ability to snap ourselves out of these states at will. Emotional intelligence translates into the capacity to acknowledge these feelings and let them move through, so we can return to a stable, balanced state quicker.

This capacity is easy to understand by the logical mind, but it is not easy to practice. As Anand says, "I wish people could become emotionally intelligent just by reading a book or listening to a lecture. Humanity would be enlightened already."

Unfortunately, this skill can only emerge through consistent practice. Meditation, supported by breathing techniques, is one of the fundamental practices to rewire the nervous system, and the kriyas help to restore the hormonal and emotional balance.

Sattva Yoga includes many approaches, as a holistic, integrative solutions to the full spectrum of a human being. For example, meditation alone works for aspects of the mind, but emotions may spill over and hijack the mind. Then we can spend the entire meditation thinking, planning, or worrying without even being aware that we are doing it or unable to stop.

That is what happened to me with the transcendental meditation practice that I learned in Hong Kong. Before I experienced breathing techniques with Anand in India, I meditated consistently for several years, but my anxiety about specific issues remained. It was hardwired in my nervous system as a default programming. When I found breathwork and kriyas in the Himalayas, I started to feel the release in my body on an emotional and neurological level, and meditation took on a new, deeper value. Also, wisdom talks from Anand helped to process many unanswered questions and calm my worried mind.

As my first teacher's training came to its conclusion, I realized that if I went back home and did nothing with these tools, eventually the old habits would creep in. I would return back to square one: angry, anxious, fearful, and egoistic. Once again, I would be fundamentally frustrated with life. I would be the one who treated happiness as a transaction of things and experiences, not an inner state. I would go back to being a person who does things on autopilot just because they were done this way before and never question the relevance of it all to my own fulfillment. Yet again, I would become addicted to stress, anger, and stimulants to feel alive.

I did not want to regress to my old self. I was determined to keep my newly found inner contentment. But how?

Two questions arose in my mind. First, *"Wow, this is all great and transformational, but would it work on people who cannot come to India and immerse themselves?"* The second question was, *"Would these practices be accepted in the business world where I felt stress and anxiety were ruining people's lives?"*

An idea came to my mind on how I could make myself accountable and keep up the practice. This realization is where my current story begins.

Notes:

_____

_____

_____

_____

_____

_____

_____

_____

_____

_____

_____

_____

_____

_____

_____

_____

_____

_____

_____

CHAPTER 6

SattvaMe:
REACH THE NEXT LEVEL

"Be ashamed to die until you scored some great victory for humanity." - Neil DeGrasse Tyson

Upon my return from India to Miami, I knew that I needed to do something different to hold myself accountable to my meditation practice. An idea came to me to offer business meditation in the coworking space where I had recently started a new job.

The setting was perfect. The office, located on the 32nd floor of a high-rise building, had an elegant conference room with huge windows and an unobstructed view overlooking the Biscayne Bay and the Atlantic Ocean. The sunrise was magnificent. All I needed was permission from my new boss to use the space.

I did not know how he would react. At the time, the idea of meditation at work was foreign. Not only had I never heard of meditation at work, but I had never done it. My strategy was to offer sessions just outside of work hours. I also decided to open it up to the entire business community in downtown Miami. My boss accepted.

To prepare, I adjusted the techniques I had learned in India to fit a business setting. I started with an explanation of the practice, why it was important, and the potential benefits of practicing meditation. I called the session "Meditation Journey." My goal was to transition the professionals from their current mental and emotional states to one of far grander value, filled with more peace, acceptance, focus, and happiness. I would also create a new intention for each class.

Thinking back on my own work experiences, I knew that it would be incredibly challenging to find the complete stillness and silence that meditation requires. Therefore, I designed a strategy to get busy professionals to slow down from their fast-paced minds to a complete stop without creating mental resistance to the practice.

Interestingly, my strategy mirrors our brain's capacity to switch brain waves. Like the gears of a car, our brain can switch from running 120 miles per hour to a full stop.

When we are in a deep sleep, our body and mind enter unconscious stillness, corresponding to the lowest delta waves. These are the waves of a deep sleep, restoration, and subconscious consolidation of everything that happened that day.

When we start to wake and enter into a half-asleep, drowsy state, our brain waves switch to theta waves, which is like a car's first gear. These are the waves of super-learning, whole-brain thinking and flow. If you have ever done hypnosis, this is the state you enter to reprogram your subconscious habits and beliefs.

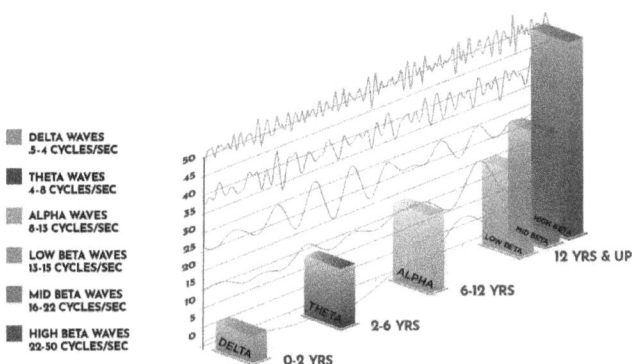

| DELTA WAVES .5-4 CYCLES/SEC |
| THETA WAVES 4-8 CYCLES/SEC |
| ALPHA WAVES 8-13 CYCLES/SEC |
| LOW BETA WAVES 13-15 CYCLES/SEC |
| MID BETA WAVES 16-22 CYCLES/SEC |
| HIGH BETA WAVES 22-50 CYCLES/SEC |

DELTA 0-2 YRS · THETA 2-6 YRS · ALPHA 6-12 YRS · LOW BETA / MID BETA / HIGH BETA 12 YRS & UP

During deep meditation, we drop into theta and delta brain waves. But instead of falling asleep, we remain awake and aware, gaining the ability to watch the content of our subconscious mind and inner world.

Watching our subconscious allows us to choose which "files" in our brain's memory bank that we want to keep and which files we want to discard. This is the essence of self-correction. The awareness also opens the capacity to release bio-memory on an emotional level, changing the hormones from stress to restoration and calmness.

It is nearly impossible to get to these brain waves on demand if you only practice through guided meditations or use meditation apps. That is why traditional meditation practice is relevant if you want to make profound changes. If you do not use unassisted self-practice (traditional meditation), over time, the subconscious programs override our finite will to change. As a result, we give up on goals and new habits like New Year's resolutions shortly after setting them.

Once we realize we can be our own hypnotists and have the power to change the contents of the subconscious mind, we become inspired to practice each day and no longer need the discipline to do it. The desire to meditate starts to come naturally, like eating or brushing our teeth.

As we get up to start the day and remain in a calm state after a good night's sleep (without yet touching our cell phone, the news, or emails), we are in alpha waves. These are the bridge between the conscious and subconscious mind. We are relaxed and remain inward, but we are also fully aware of the outside environment. In this state, we process the inputs that come from the external world, and we decide whether they make sense. Then we choose which information we want to keep or forget. Alpha waves are responsible for creativity, intuitive insight, a sense of connection, and learning.

In meditation, when accessing alpha waves, we feel deeply relaxed and expansive. Most guided meditations and apps will get us here with ease. That is why mindfulness and meditation relieve stress. Ultimately, these tools activate the parasympathetic nervous system, balancing short- and long-term stress—a chronic disease of the business world.

As adults, we spend most of our time in beta waves when we place full awareness on the outside world. There are three levels of beta waves: low, mid, and high. In low beta, we are active and alert. We also more easily switch from low beta to alpha, allowing us to respond to external stimuli and do it in a way that is more creative and long-term oriented.

As the stress and the pace of life increases, our brain speeds up and shifts to higher gears—the mid-beta waves. In my experience, mid-beta correlates to the subtle feelings of anxiety, mild frustration, and dissatisfaction, but we cannot point out where these feelings originated. Sadly, most people spend their waking hours in mid-beta. We focus on doing things, moving fast, and checking off lists, but we are not necessarily feeling fulfilled. Living in mid-beta is what I call "120-miles-per-hour mode." It is a relevant state for short spurts of time under certain life situations; however, it damages the brain if sustained for long periods of time.

High-beta are waves of extreme stress, anger, and rage. This is when we go into full panic mode or mental and emotional burnout. We lose our ability to respond to external stimuli and start reacting; we can be triggered by any little thing. When we are in high-beta, we are moving at 160 miles per hour and spinning.

Lastly, there are the highest frequency waves—the gamma waves. They correlate to genius insight, natural ecstasy, and spiritual, mystical experiences. The business world does not have much grounds for these waves to arise. Most people would need psychedelics to enter these states at least once in a lifetime.

In India, we would induce gamma waves through various breathing techniques and kriyas, which feels sublime, joyful, and infinite. These are deeply healing for our being waves, when arise naturally.

While scientists and doctors use EEG technology to

measure all these waves, it is complex to do it in a real-life scenario. Meditation affords us a visceral understanding and experience of the brain waves and how they shift during the day. With consistent practice, we gain the capacity to switch them on demand, down-regulating or up-regulating our mental activity appropriate to the situation. The ability to switch between brain waves is the essence of self-mastery.

During my first meditation class at the coworking space, the room was filled. I was both thrilled and intimidated. I recognized a couple of people from the building while others were new. The majority of attendees had never meditated before, but they had a sincere interest to learn.

After briefly introducing the benefits of meditation, I set an intention for the class and then started guiding everyone with gentle movements used to create body awareness and the mind-body connection. Naturally, at first everyone was uncomfortable, but as we progressed, I could feel the anxiety melting away.

As we switched from breathing techniques into the guided meditation, the sun was rising, illuminating the room with a magical, golden glow.

After a few minutes, I realized that the woman to my left was crying. I thought, *"Oh my, what have I done wrong?"* I worked internally on remaining calm while dealing with my insecurity. It was all too new for me, and I did not know how to respond. Since she was in a deep meditative state, I decided to let her be. I placed a tissue box next to her and concentrated on guiding the group deep into the experience.

After the practice, everyone was filled with a sense of calm and clarity. People were thanking me and sharing how much they enjoyed it and how wonderful they felt. They were determined to come back.

The woman on my left stayed. She came up to me with a deep sense of gratitude in her eyes. Her dad had passed away eight months ago, and while she was sad, she did not have the ability to release her emotions. During the meditation, the grief had bubbled to the surface and she felt a sense of relief, which was why she was crying.

My heart expanded with the realization of the level of impact meditation could deliver. Not just because meditation is a stress-relief and productivity tool but also because meditation helps us go through human experiences, like pain, loss, and confusion. This woman had been holding onto the trauma of her loss for months, and within a half-hour practice, she had the emotional release she was unable to get before. No surprise, she became a regular meditator.

After two months of weekly morning meditation sessions and people sharing with me the impact they felt, I became inspired. I knew I had found a passion and meaning in service on a level I had not experienced before. I asked myself *"Would teaching meditation and mindfulness be something I could do for the rest of my life?"* I heard a loud YES inside my head and heart.

With research, I realized that meditation and mindfulness tools were starting to get attention and creating a business around the idea was possible.

This concept gave me the confidence to expand my meditation journey offering to other companies, events, and organizations around South Florida. It took me about six months to erase any remaining doubts in my skeptical mind that the techniques were relevant in the business environment.

My husband, who saw my transformation and growth firsthand, agreed to back me and fund the business for as long as needed to get it profitable. I quit my job, and after my second teacher training session in the Indian Himalayas, I founded SattvaMe—a Mindfulness + Meditation training company for personal and leadership development.

"Sattva" in Sanskrit means qualities of balance, calmness, steadiness, goodness, and harmony. A holistic and energy-rich way of existing is the golden middle between a chaotic and dull life. Only from these sattvic qualities of consciousness can we permanently transform, feel happy, and impact others and the world on a grand collective level.

The company name *SattvaMe* means to *make me whole again*. *SattvaMe* has the intention of awakening wholeness in each leader, entrepreneur, and executive to live a fulfilling life on all levels of existence—mental, physical, emotional, and spiritual. Once we feel whole and fulfilled inside, we open up to the next level of our innate capacity for peak performance to serve and uplift others. From the top, the spirit of service and greater good trickles down to the rest of the organization.

What stops us from being our whole self every minute of our lives? Mostly, a combination of stress, fear, and old habits. Practicing mindfulness and meditation has the potential to turn stress to contentment and success. As *New York Times* best-selling author and meditator Michael Singer brilliantly states, "[c]hallenging situations create the force needed to bring about change. The problem is that we generally use all the stirred-up energy intended to bring about change to resist change."

A lack of education about human functioning on a mental, emotional, and spiritual level enables stress to create disease and dysfunction within our personal and professional lives. But the same energy of stress can be used to support growth.

Once I realized that stress could be used for positive change, I started to view it as this powerful force that we can channel to our benefit. Applied to the business world, the changes are exponential.

Scientists have done an incredible job shedding light on the biology of stress, the functioning of the human brain, and psychology. However, this knowledge alone is incomplete without practical tools and clear instructions on how to apply them.

Science also cannot yet define and explain the incredible power of energy that created the universe, Earth, and life. We all feel this energy field, but in the business world, we shy away from talking about it, never mind using it for growth and transformation.

In my opinion, the most revolutionary research on energy and spirituality is the one about the flow state. According to the book *Flow* by Mihaly Csikszentmihalyi, the flow state is the study of "positive human experiences—such as joy, creativity, and the process of total involvement with life." In business, flow translates to the optimal state for high peak performance and productivity, followed by a sense of fulfillment and intrinsic motivation.

Csikszentmihalyi does not shy away from attributing the flow state to our idea of the meaning in life. According to his research, we all look for a flow state in some way to find the purpose of our existence. However, for most people, the experiences of joy and engagement are random and not replicable.

Some of the flow state attributes are a distortion of time, loss of body and self-awareness, effortlessness, a sense of unity, supreme creativity, and superb problem-solving. In my life, before mindfulness and meditation, I felt the flow in nature while doing sports and crafts and sometimes in the night-clubs. However, these were spontaneous experiences that I could not replicate on demand until I established regular meditation practice.

Most research up until now has studied the flow states in extreme sports and with athletes, which does not translate into business and life scenarios. Even as I write this book, there is still not a lot of verified research on the flow state induced through mediation.

In my experience and the experience of other advanced meditators, we can enter the flow state on demand

and use it as a tool for high mental performance and creativity. Using flow always proceeds from an unbounded amount of joy and fulfillment, even though there might be psychological and physical tiredness present as well. It becomes part of everyday life and therefore is more potent and accessible for business professionals.

However, meditation practice must be consistent and done for a prolonged period of time before we can gain the capacity for mental and emotional regulation at will. It also cannot be accessed through apps and guided meditation. We need to learn to meditate on our own to become familiar with the different aspects of the mind and emotions on an intimate level.

With short attention spans, many people do not commit to a 20- to 30-minute meditation and instead opt for a 10-minute app recording. While a 10-minute meditation has relaxation benefits, it is not enough to gain self-realization and self-mastery.

I have learned my formal meditation practice from Anand while training in the Himalayas. It is a simple, time-tested technique. To meet the skepticism of logical, business-oriented minds, I combine it with scientific evidence and explanations.

SattvaMe Meditation Initiation is a multi-day process followed by a month of consultative follow-ups. Due to specific rules and respect for the Vedic Himalayan tradition, it is not something I can share in a book. (To learn more about SattvaMe Meditation Initiation, please go to www.sattva.me and inquire about the NextLevel 1:1 Packages).

To start immediately, use the mindfulness meditation technique below, which is easy to practice anywhere, any-time, for as long or as little as you feel comfortable.

SELF-PRACTICE MINDFULNESS TOOL:

Find your most comfortable seated position and start to pay attention to your breathing. Instead of breathing on purpose, notice how your breathing naturally happens. Follow the breath until it becomes subtle and hard to follow. Then remain in stillness and silence for as long as possible. Expect that something will draw your attention, like thoughts, feelings, or body sensations. When you realized it happened, simply return to the breathing and start over.

Going in and out of the meditative state, created by the breath, and mind wandering away from it, is like going to the gym to strengthen your mental and emotional muscles. It is best if you practice for at least 10–15 minutes to experience 3–4 cycles of you getting into a quiet space. This allows you to catch your mind wandering, as well as your reactions to it.

With time, you will notice how this ability to "catch the mind-wandering" during meditation will translate into a skill that you can use while at work and going about your life.

It is a frequent question to me on which industry SattvaMe works with the most. In my experience, there is no particular industry, company size, or profession where mindfulness tools work best. SattvaMe focuses on professionals who want to reach the next level in their mental, emotional, and spiritual evolution. We energize them to win in their craft by sustaining peak performance and conscious leadership. We have done workshops for leadership teams in Fortune 500 companies as well as small businesses, and one-on-one coaching with entrepreneurs and leaders, nationwide and globally.

The best "students" share a fundamental desire that nudges them to see these practices as the gateway to evolution and higher meaning. They know that despite their business successes, there is something more to life, and they are willing to question the normality of stress in our society and explore spirituality. Without this slight dissatisfaction, I have seen people fall off meditation practice and return to their old selves.

Those that invest in their evolution know that it is a difficult path with no shortcuts. But it is the only path to a meaningful life. To get started, we need an expert that we trust, and patience with the process.

With SattvaMe, I am honored and aspire to be one of these role models for others who are interested in transformation. Being in mindfulness and meditation business holds me accountable to practice every day with joy and a sense of purpose for the good of humanity.

As part of social responsibility, SattvaMe works with prisons, including high-security facilities, to educate incarcerated men and women on the benefits of the daily mindfulness practice. We partake in programs that help them integrate back into society as active citizens when released.

At SattvaMe, our purpose is *to energize leaders to win in their craft.* Through Mindfulness + Meditation techniques, we elevate consciousness to the next level. Higher consciousness means not mindlessly completing tasks but creating greater awareness of why we are doing them, how to derive more meaning and joy from the process, and positively impact others and the world.

At SattvaMe, we train leaders and their teams on the aspects of mental and emotional flexibility to reach and sustain peak performance, regardless of external circumstances. We give practical mindfulness tools to reach the next level in their leadership, team, and organizational culture.

While the fundamental knowledge comes from the Himalayan ancient wisdom, we back it up by the scientific explanations from neuroscience, psychology, quantum physics, and business practicality. With SattvaMe techniques, busy executives access flow state and creativity on demand by training and reconditioning the mind.

Stress brings about the challenge that is needed to activate the energy to make a change. Meditation stimulates parts of the brain that allows us to avoid triggering a fight-or-flight response to resist change and instead enter into a flow, a state of creative problem solving. As a result, professionals feel more joy and fulfillment, which leads to intrinsic motivation to work more holistically and for the good of humanity. What a shift from the mentality of the past!

How to get there? Practice and patience.

CHAPTER 7

BE PATIENT

"There is no rhythm without a pause."
- A common saying

It was a Saturday morning in 2010, a few years before fleeing Miami for Hong Kong and losing my dad. I woke up with the same sense of urgency that I experienced during the week. My heart raced with the all-too-familiar mild anxiety. So much to do, so little time!

Rushing through my morning routine and grabbing breakfast on the go (a frequent ritual), I headed north for my hair appointment. With my phone in one hand and the steering wheel in the other, I approached the junction of 395 and I-95, one of the busiest intersections in Miami, at about 60 miles per hour.

Maybe I was going too slow or perhaps I was wiggling on the road. I only remember how the pick-up truck driver behind me sharply swerved around me and then purposefully hit the brakes so that I had to slam my own to avoid a collision. The next few seconds moved slowly, as if an eternity had gone by.

My light Suzuki Forenza started to swing left and right

uncontrollably and then spun 360 degrees from the right side of the highway all the way to the left, across five lanes of traffic. I was desperately trying to regain control of the car. By a sheer miracle, it did not hit any of the other vehicles speeding by me. I continued spinning until the car abruptly stopped two feet from the concrete road divider, facing ongoing traffic.

My heart was jumping out of my throat. I was shaking and gasping for air. Tears were running down my face. My phone flew behind the passenger seat where I could no longer reach it. It was a miracle that I did not have a single scratch or damage to my body, the car, nor anyone on the road. But now I was in another pickle—I was facing oncoming traffic off the express lane.

For a few minutes, I tried to stabilize my nerves and clear my thoughts, but it was hard as I was watching cars going 70 miles per hour right at me. I was parked on the curb, but it was too small, and drivers still needed to pay attention to go around my car. If one did not, we would crash. The view of the road was obstructed because of a hump ahead of me. *How could I find the only hill in flat Florida?* A question that I still ask myself to this day.

Every single driver was blowing their horn at me and throwing hands in the air with anger. *How do you think I got here?* I kept asking them in my head. It was nerve-racking and dangerous to stay in the same spot. I wished for a police car or a tow truck, but there was none in sight.

I made an attempt to turn around, but limited visibility, sharp angles, and the high speed of oncoming traffic made it impossible. Eventually, I realized that I needed to come closer to the median to gain the visibility I needed to find a gap to turn around.

This was not my first car accident caused by distractions. Just a few weeks prior, I ran into the bumper of the car in front of me because I was texting and driving while in slow traffic. It became clear that my impatience and desire to multitask were threatening my life and the lives of others.

> According to the National Highway Traffic Safety Administration, texting is the most common and dangerous distraction. "Sending or reading a text takes your eyes off the road for five seconds. At 55 mph, that's like driving the length of an entire football field with your eyes closed!"

> In 2016, 3,450 people were killed in motor vehicle crashes. Nineteen percent of fatal crashes were reported as distraction-affected crashes. Distraction could be anything that takes away attention—phone, radio/entertainment, passengers, and other drivers. In 2015 alone, 391,000 people were injured in motor vehicle crashes involving distracted drivers. And these numbers have increased by 5-to-9 percent from previous years.

Everyone knows that texting and driving is dangerous. We are not stupid, nor do we wish to die and hurt others on purpose. Then why do we still text and drive? My answer is that we lack patience and have become addicted to distraction. We have lost the ability to focus on routine tasks, and now society pays a high price for this inattention. Most accidents and deaths on the road could be easily avoided if we were more patient and attentive while driving.

Impatience is cultivated by technology, social media, and a culture of fast transactions. Distracted behavior gets enforced by the hormones in our brain. When we get a text, email, or any other notification on our phones or other devices, our brain releases dopamine, known as the reward and pleasure hormone. As per nature's design, dopamine is a great motivational mechanism that makes us work harder and longer for a reward. Now, technology companies have figured out how to release dopamine more frequently to make their devices and apps highly addictive. Sounds, colors, fast motion, sense of achievement—all contribute to the addiction. The same strategy is used in gambling. The dopamine rush is so powerful that we cannot resist the urge to press the button and check our phone again and again—in meetings, during a meal, and while driving.

Mildly drugged by the hormones of our own body, we now crave the pleasure of distraction and strive to avoid the pain of boredom. Take away a phone from a teenager and you see addiction withdrawal in action. Or even better, turn off your own phone for a weekend and count how many times you want to check it. It is a painful experience, but I highly recommend it. When I suggest this to my clients, I cannot help but smile at their panicked face expressions.

We value high performance and multitasking so much that we believe it is a waste of time to do one thing when instead we can do several things at once. Unfortunately, multitasking is a myth. Science has proven over and over again that our brain consciously can only focus on one thing at a time.

Let's test it now. Look around for anything red. Go ahead. Look around for five seconds for the color red. Done?

Now, as you read this sentence, think about everything you saw that was blue. What about anything that was green? I bet it is not as easy to remember things you saw that were blue or green, as opposed to the red items you had focused on. When I do this exercise in my workshop, people usually have puzzled expressions as they realize they failed to "multi-task" when they focused on finding red-colored items.

Multitasking is nothing but a fast switch between tasks, which unnecessarily exhausts the brain, burns more energy, and makes us tired faster. Not only we are accomplishing less, but the quality of our work suffers.

According to an IBM study that surveyed 1,500 executives, creativity is the most desired skill for successful CEOs, not multitasking as young executives aspire to believe. Yet, surrounded by our lifeless, concrete skies, tight suits, and rubber-soled, unconductive shoes, we are more ungrounded and scattered in our minds than ever before. "If you have been using your brain to multitask—as most of us do most of the day—and then you set that aside and go on a walk, without all of the gadgets, you have let the prefrontal cortex recover," says researcher David Strayer of the University of Utah. "And that's when we see these bursts in creativity, problem-solving, and feelings of well-being."

You can say, *But I am able to drive and talk on the phone at the same time, no?* Correct, and that is because you use two different parts of the brain. It is only possible to do two things at once if you pair a routine, learned subconscious behavior with one that requires us to be conscious and alert. When we already know how to drive well, so we switch on the autopilot of our subconscious moving brain—cerebellum—while the alert and aware part of our brain—the prefrontal cortex—focuses on the conversation.

Now, do you remember when you first learned how to drive before it became habitual? How comfortable were you talking on the phone or texting at the same time then? Or why do you need to lower the radio volume when looking for a new address?

Sadly, people now attempt to do 2–5 activities at the same time, which all require acute attention. We write an email, while talking on the phone, while signaling someone to come to our office for a conversation and finishing lunch. All at once. This is madness. This is an epidemic of distraction and lack of efficiency. We end up busy and tired, not more productive. And our communication and ability to relate to each other suffers.

We forget that high sustainable performance only comes with repetitive tireless routine practice and by focusing on one task at a time. Think of admired athletes, artists, or business professionals. They will verify that they have spent thousands of hours practicing and testing routines to make them automatic before they became successful. This is patience in action that leads to self-mastery. Unfortunately, it is a skill few have.

The good news is that patience and focus are trainable skills. During meditation, for example, almost everyone experiences an impulse to do something else rather than sit still. The training happens when we choose not to respond to what the mind and emotions tell us to do and, instead, we remain still. If you did the self-practice mindfulness technique from the previous chapter, how did it feel?

In meditation, you may want to scratch, move, and get up. Thoughts come in. It feels uncomfortable. Now you know that this is only the conditioned body craving a dopamine hit. By telling it to settle down, you regain your personal power. The trick is not to obey your urge for distraction and instead continue with the task of sitting still, relaxing into the discomfort.

These uncomfortable feelings and sensations mean change. Eventually, you start noticing how much easier and more enjoyable meditation becomes. The dopamine craving will be replaced with the release of serotonin—the happy hormone—which regulates mood and emotions, among other functions. You will know that meditation is working once you feel more patience in day-to-day life, especially when you are used to losing your temper and attention.

Self-mastery of this kind is important to stay relevant in our fast-changing times. Historian, philosopher, and best-selling author Yuval Noah Harari predicts that evolution in technology will be disrupting the job market at an exponential rate. "Nobody knows what the job market will look like in 2040," he says. He means that whatever your profession is now, it may become irrelevant in 10 years. And then whatever you learned new at that time to adapt will again become irrelevant in another 10 years, and so on. Many professions will not exist. New professions will emerge, and we better have the patience to learn them in order to stay relevant.

The best investment you can make right now is to develop mental flexibility, mental balance, and emotional intelligence. Being a master of yourself will stay in high demand especially in fast-changing times. "How to keep changing throughout life; how to keep learning throughout life? We don't have a college degree in change," says Harari, "but these are the most important tools."

One of my secrets for gaining more patience, besides

meditation, is embracing the mantra "This Too Shall Pass" from King Solomon. This phrase reminds me that everything changes and is not as important as it seems. The most painful experiences and difficult projects will pass; so will the most positive and desired. It is a universal truth. This mental reminder expands patience, resilience, and joy. It also helps relax goals and let go of judgments, which are the leading cause of anxiety.

Sometimes, we are so wrapped up in our anxiety about the future that we forget that life is temporary. Reminding ourselves of this simple fact helps us to slow down and reflect more on what is really important. That's why in Buddhist traditions, one of the techniques to quiet the mind and emotions is to meditate on death. Once we remember that life is a temporary arrangement, certain things lose urgency and importance.

Hold on, you may say, *if I relax too much, I won't be successful.* Up until recently, I deeply embraced this thinking. I pushed and I worked harder than others to the point where my passion and commitment were almost interpreted as aggression and stubbornness. What I learned is that there is no need for such uncompromising pressure in life. When you embrace flow, life becomes easier and produces better outcomes.

The traditional "work hard to reach your goal" model has become a source of anxiety and unhappiness. First, we decide that we want a certain outcome, let's say a promotion. Then we pick a point in time by which we estimate we would get it. Usually, this timeline is short, because we are impatient to get to the outcome or we do not set realistic expectations. Today's young workforce, for example, now estimates to reach a senior position within 1–2 years.

Successful people know that everything always takes longer than we think. As Bill Gates once said, "[m]ost people overestimate what they can do in one year and underestimate what they can do in 10 years."

We set the imaginary timelines, assuming that all the conditions should align as per our plan. Naturally, life does not go according to our plans. We miss our self-imposed timelines, which leads to unhappiness with the present situation. We get frustrated, demotivated, judgmental, doubtful, and less patient because now we also lost the sense of trust in ourselves, others, and life in general. No wonder today's career paths look like a zigzag line rather than the straight-line trajectory of career paths a few decades ago.

Even as I write this book, according to my own ambitious timelines, I should have finished by now, but I have not. I can feel the pressure and anxiety accumulate in the area of my chest and shoulders.

In the past, I would soliloquize on how I was not working hard enough, my ideas were not good enough, and I was falling behind schedule. Instead, I now recognize this pattern and can break it. I consciously choose to override my demotivating thoughts and praise myself for contributing to my long-desired dream to be an author. I trust that with consistent input, this project will get done and that *This Too Shall Pass.*

I also realized that my timelines were too short, and I have replaced them with more relaxed goals. After talking to first-time book authors, I was able to gain my confidence back and create a new belief: *Put in the effort consistently, relax about time, trust the process, the outcome will come.* As anxiety arises, I relax into it, instead of fighting it. The fact that you are reading this book is living proof that this strategy works. And I started and published the book within one year!

Living on deadlines is so deeply ingrained in me that it requires constant awareness and self-correction to consciously release it. This book became my practice to be more patient with myself and silence the inner critic. What I found is that I now enjoy writing and look forward to it.

I am not saying that setting goals is useless. Goals are important vehicles for progress when used correctly. I suggest that we stop the self-induced dissatisfaction and judgment. If you think about it, self-criticism is unhealthy and destructive. We create timelines by the construct of our logical mind, based on experiences that could never be replicated in the exact same way, and enforce them through societal pressures that do not always have our best interest at heart.

Once we become aware of this simple fact, it is easier to reverse back to freedom. If you are responsible, hardworking, and enthusiastic about what you do, you will reach your goal. How long will it take? No one has control over the timeline. It is up to you to change and adjust the timeline as your unpredictable life unfolds. I once heard a quote from entrepreneur and speaker Barrett Ersek on how "not to confuse vision with distance! The vision is brighter than ever; the distance is just a little further than we thought."

Impatience is nothing but resistance to boredom arising from a lack of purpose. We all want more peace and stability, but when we slow down, we feel bored and anxious because there is nothing to fill the gap, nothing to excite us. The body that is used to constant adrenaline or dopamine rush, starts to crave the stimuli. To avoid the pain, most pick up the pace again and engage in mindless behavior to check out.

When we operate on autopilot, it seems like a lot is happening in a day and we feel "busy." Eventually, we normalize even the strongest hormones in our body and start to mindlessly skim through life. We eat fast, work fast, interact fast, and react fast as if we are on a program. We go through the motions of life without putting much thought into the essence of why we do the things we do in the first place and how we could do them differently to gain happiness. Naturally, we lose patience and become frustrated when life does not go according to plan. Does this sound familiar at all?

With meditation, we break the cycle. We intentionally and consistently put our lives on pause and revise its content. Our mind wants to check out or do something else, but we pull it back into the present moment and what is important for us. At first, it feels uncomfortable and unnatural. Our bodies crave the familiar hormone patterns causing self-critical emotions and confusion.

We do not like to see the mental and emotional mess most of us have been living in for so long.

Why endure the pain when we can just keep going? Because it does not serve us well. Remember, statistics show that distracted driving is the leading cause of most car accidents. Other research shows that people whose minds wander and check out of the present moment are less happy than people who stay present and engaged with work and life. When we are distracted, we are more likely to react when triggered and say things we later regret. Overall, our quality of life and relationships suffer. As we meditate, our quality of presence and patience expands.

I started my practice before the "app-mania" with self-guided mantra-meditation (more widely known as transcendental meditation). It was hard because I watched how bored and impatient my mind would grow without anything to pull me out of the downward spiral. Observing my mind wander forced me to learn how to switch from that state because it was unbearable to experience it. Fighting anxiety arising from seeing my patterns would only make things worse.

As we discussed in the previous chapter, when we are impatient or resistant to anything that happens in life, we use stirred-up energy to fight the change. This energy can flow freely or get stuck. Since change is constant, we simply waste our inner resources on anxiety, complaining or worrying. It does not add much to life, but we feel like we gain something because we blow steam. How could we make better use of this energy?

Patience is the process of liberating "stuckness" and embracing change. Patience supports mental agility, flexibility, growth, and evolution. Instead of constantly fighting life, we can get in the flow with it. For that to happen, we must exercise relaxing into a state of being present with kindness and compassion towards self and others. In other words, we must be more patient.

AWARENESS TOOL:

Make a list of situations where you lose patience—perhaps in traffic, while waiting in line, or any particular times at work or with family. Think of repeated behavior rather than a one-time scenario.

- Now that you are aware of your pattern, remember what happens in your body. Where do you hold the tension?
- With the awareness you just gained, could you choose a different thought, feeling, or behavior to change the outcome that leads to more calmness and happiness?

Meditation helps create self-awareness to catch yourself in the moment. Until you develop this skill through regular practice, try to gain awareness by asking for help and observations from close friends and family.

A few suggestions:

- Ask a friend, family member, or colleague to point out the pattern you want to change when you fall into it next time.

- Remember it yourself and do the opposite of what you usually do (if you get mad - laugh; if you get tight - relax; etc.).
- Put a Post-it note or an alarm on your phone to keep yourself present.
- Compliment yourself each time when you are able to change the pattern.
- Keep repeating reinforcement until you condition a new desired behavior.

The closest I can describe being fully aware of the flow with life is a state of expansion. When we are impatient, bored, or anxious, we contract, physically and mentally. Remember the last argument you had with your loved one? How did the area of your chest or stomach feel— opened or closed? How did it feel emotionally—light or heavy?

Feelings of kindness, gratitude, and compassion towards ourselves and others allow us to feel light and expansive. The expansion gives us energy and patience. This is the only sure way to freedom and stability. When you face pain or change, expand from it in order to break free. Otherwise, all you are doing is fighting life. Guess who wins?

Mindfulness and meditation can be used to train feelings of expansion. All you need to do is pay attention to the space around you, away from the body. Notice everything and nothing in particular. It feels liberating too.

Since I started to be more mindful of my behavior, I have noticed the need to change my mental dialogue. Becoming intentional helped me go from boredom to engagement, from anger to appreciation, even in the most routine tasks. I also put an exciting purpose behind my actions.

For example, when driving, my purpose is to keep myself and everyone around me safe. I feel good and virtuous about it. Texting is against that value. I ask myself, *Is this text or email so urgent that it is worth a life?* A bit extreme, but it keeps me sharp and interested in driving rather than multitasking, like being on the phone.

To avoid distraction, it is important to keep your mind occupied with something fun and meaningful. I keep my mind happy by listening to a podcast or staying in meditative silence to reflect on my day. Because I am learning and contemplating, I no longer consider driving a waste of time, so I do not regress to using my phone.

The best part is that I have not been involved in a car accident since I started practicing mindfulness and meditation. In fact, the dreadful spin on the highway I described earlier serves as a reminder and motivation to practice more when I feel impatient.

Notes:

_____

_____

_____

_____

_____

_____

_____

_____

_____

_____

_____

_____

_____

_____

_____

_____

_____

CHAPTER 8
DAILY PRACTICE

"Most of us can't handle uncomfortable self-examination."
- Ryan Holiday

Looking back at my life, I am one of the lucky ones to break the bondage from the insane egocentric tendency for negativity, victimization, self-sabotage, guilt, shame, loneliness, chronic dissatisfaction, unworthiness, and fluctuation with arrogance and entitlement. It is not an easy journey, and I still feel vulnerable on my "bad days." Little by little, as I let go of these conditioned behaviors, I experience more freedom, peace, joy, gratitude, confidence, clarity, love, unity, connection, and acceptance of what is, not what I wish it to be.

If I let go of my practice, I can relapse like an addict after years of not touching the "substance." Our addictions of the mind are more powerful than we give them credit. It is not an overnight transformation but a consistent day-to-day choice. I attribute making better choices to my daily routine and continuous practice to create more space and flow for being and less doing.

Since I found Sattva Retreat and Anand, I have barely

missed a day without conscious practice. Doing so, I correct my intellect every day and help my mind and body release old memories, traumas, and emotions that hold me back from experiencing a full life. Without the wisdom and guidance of my teachers and the support of my husband and friends, I would self-sabotage many times over and quit when times get very rough.

We are creatures of habits and rituals. Consuming news, which is mostly negative, is a ritual. Checking social media, which creates unrealistic comparisons, is a habit. Using food, alcohol, and other stimulants to numb the emotional pain of loneliness and isolation are collective behaviors in our culture.

The solution is to counterbalance limiting habits with more supportive rituals and habits in our lives. In my experience and through the experience of my clients, when we turn our first morning and last evening hours into a nurturing routine, the rest of the day flows. When each day flows, our whole life flows and is filled with meaning, fulfillment, and abundance that each of us seeks.

Here I want to share with you my daily routine in hope to inspire and energize you to do incremental changes in your life. By adding more mindfulness, meditation, and other supportive habits you too can reach the NEXT LEVEL YOU.

MY DAILY ROUTINE

I set my alarm to around 5–6 am, even when traveling. Rising early is a choice and a trained skill. If I let my old self take over, I would be sleeping till 9 or 10 am and wake up angry and restless. Early morning is also the quietest part of the day for meditation with supportive energy and less distractions.

Once I get out of bed, the first thing I do is drink 12–16 ounces of room-temperature water, which I prepare the night before. After a quick bathroom visit, I head to my home office, which is also my space for meditation practice. Since I am up early, I allow myself up to two hours to practice the tools and techniques to help me reach the next level.

First, I start with a Puja ritual, which I learned in India. It is a mindful, devotional ritual that assists in refining the limiting state of consciousness and replaces it with one of grander, supportive values of gratitude and unity. Puja puts me in a state of receptivity, presence of grace, and wholeness. It is especially powerful for women and brings positive energy to the space where you practice. It is a combination of specific mantras and offerings to the five elements (water, earth, fire, air, and ether) used to create the desired state in the person performing the Puja. The whole process takes about 15 minutes.

Next, I transition to a spinal series and stretches to support and heal my back while listening to calm music, an audiobook or podcast. With all the stress and anxiety dominating my past life, I have a herniated disk in L4/L5. These exercises give me a greater range of motion and nearly eliminate the pain without the support of drugs.

After the body work, I sit on a cushion facing East, a

suggested cardinal direction for morning meditation practice that symbolizes light, energy, positivity, vitality, and the new beginnings with the rising of the sun.

First, I do a series of breathing exercises to raise my energy and clear my mind. Breathing creates an alkaline environment in the body, balancing oxygen and CO_2 levels. Combined with precise body movements and sounds, these breathing exercises stimulate the bio-memory release of past traumas and conditioning. All leads to a deeper meditation experience, which I drop into for at least a half hour right after the exercise set.

Around 7 or 7:30 am, I go to give and receive the warmest, longest hug from my husband and our loving dog, Lola, who we squeeze between us in a triple-hug. We all look forward to this family ritual, especially Lola, as she waits for us to pick her up for the hug.

Then we all go downstairs for breakfast. Breakfast is the first time I pick up my phone to look through my calendar for the day and go through messages from the prior evening. During breakfast, we play fun or relaxing music; we do not watch TV or news.

Unless I have client meetings or travel, at 8:30 or 9 am, I leave to the office to start my workday. First, I center myself by closing my eyes and taking a few deep breaths. Then I mentally identify the three priorities that I will focus on that day. These are a must to complete tasks contributing to a grander vision for SattvaMe and for myself as a leader. I have an accountability partner with whom I report every evening on if these were completed.

In the past, my calendar was jam-packed. Now, I leave a lot of empty spaces so I can respond to any important and urgent matters and not be caught up in the minutiae. I also schedule "clarity breaks" between the meetings, which is a time for reflection, follow-up, and reset for the next meeting or task.

I recently learned that having empty space on the calendar is one of the things that "ridiculously successful people do every day" according to author Kevin Kruse. He interviewed over 200 ultra-successful people, including seven billionaires, 13 Olympians, and several successful entrepreneurs.

Another fact revealed from these interviews is that successful people have consistent morning rituals, which included nurturing the body, drinking water, and meditation, among other things like journaling, prayer, reading, eating a healthy breakfast, and light exercise.

In his book *Tools of Titans*, the best-selling author and meditator Tim Ferriss reported that meditation is the number one repeated habit among extraordinary people he interviewed.

For me, using examples from people I respect is necessary to create a disciplined practice before it becomes a habit. That is why teachers and leaders play such a huge role in our transformation. And with the internet, we can follow their lives and best practices on our own terms.

Meditation is a great energy booster during the day. Since I stopped drinking caffeine, I know that at around 2–3 pm, my focus and energy will drop and I will feel a brain fog. This is the time when I usually do a 30- to 45-minute workout or a 10- to 20-minute meditation, depending on how I feel. Both give me the juice and clarity to stay sharp and productive until the evening.

To finish my workday, I sit down for another 5- to 20-minute meditation, where I allow my tiredness and busy energy to settle down. This practice serves as a transition and prepares me for the evening ahead with family or alone. The slight degree of separation between work and home time keeps me from dragging work issues into my family life.

Professionals always ask me to speak about work-life balance, and this is exactly my answer. We must develop a strong personal practice to train our mind to be fully present. At work, it translates to being present with important tasks and not allowing the distractions to steal our awareness and attention. At home, we must give ourselves permission to be fully present with family, friends, and allocate time to rest and have fun. If we think about work after hours, we do not get enough rest. Then at the workplace, we get easily distracted, making it hard to find balance. Half-presence everywhere only leads to dissatisfaction, stress, and a lack of performance.

How can we be fully present? Mindfulness and meditation are practices that train this quality. With today's culture of always being online, it is more important than ever to create this personal culture of keeping things separate for grander awareness and happiness in all aspects of life.

Shortly after I close my workday, I go for a walk, sit in the yard, or exercise. I cook and eat dinner, mostly at home, with my husband. Then I catch up with friends or social media, watch a movie, take a bath or do a puzzle. It is important that I give myself time to do the things I enjoy as opposed to doing things that I "have to do."

One hour before bedtime, which is about 9-10 pm, I no longer use technology (phone, computer, TV). All are highly stimulating for the brain and interfere with melatonin production, a hormone responsible for a good night's sleep. I also dim all the bright lights in the house, especially in the bedroom, as light is another huge influence on our sleep patterns.

All LED lights are stimulating. I use soft yellow light, candles, and a Himalayan salt lamp instead. The brighter the light, the more awake we get. Scientific research states that we now sleep at least 3 hours less than our ancestors a century ago. Less rest translates to higher stress and less emotional resilience.

A few times a week, I enjoy a warm bath, which is relaxing and stress relieving. There is something about heat at night that stimulates better sleep. Both science and ancient wisdom suggests waking up with cold showers in the morning and winding down with a warm shower, bath, steam room, or sauna at night. I do both from time to time.

Within this hour before bed, I put on relaxing music, light candles, and meditate again for however long feels good. Sometimes I read a few pages of poetry (my favorite is Rumi) or anything relaxing and lie down to sleep. I usually doze off cuddling with my husband and our dog, Lola—another wonderful family ritual and tradition we all enjoy.

On the weekends, I keep the same morning and evening rituals. The content during the day changes, compared to the week flow, and may include work, chores, errands, and social time.

Reading this, you might think: *She is a saint. There is no way I can let go of my habit to watch TV at night while having a few drinks. And not watching or reading news? Is she a cave-woman?* Some of you have children, some like to go out, some are workaholics and answer emails 24/7. The interesting part is that I was all of this in the past (except for children). Nor am I perfect. I also answer emails at night and watch a movie from time to time. But that is a rare occasion now, not a habit. I make it a conscious choice and not a burning necessity. You can too!

IT DOESN'T FEEL RIGHT

According to Albert Einstein, "the definition of insanity is doing the same thing over and over again and expecting different results." While most people agree with Einstein, we remain incapable of making a different choice because *it doesn't feel right.*

So, let's look at what doesn't feel right? It is the

subconscious conditioning such as habits, beliefs, thoughts, and stories that may conflict with our willpower to change. Often, we are not aware of this subconscious conditioning, so it overrides the decisions we make by our conscious mind.

Meditation, breathing, and the other practical tools we have discussed in this book are designed to give us access to our subconscious contents while increasing our energy and willpower to change. That is why practices like meditation and breathing are so effective.

Changing from an unbalanced lifestyle to one of balance is not an easy endeavor. The hardest part of changing is when our subconscious conditioning starts interrupting, saying *Start tomorrow!*, or it gives us discomfort via hormones to the point where change *literally does not feel right*. This is our subconscious mind resisting change, as it likes routines, even the ones that do not lead to well-being. Habits are normal human phenomenons and are exactly what holds us back from evolving if we are not aware of them.

In the beginning, I made a game of "not trusting myself" to help me make the change. I realized that if *it didn't feel right*, it was a sign that I was on the right track to changing a pattern. I would relax into the discomfort, mentally and physically, and tell my inner voice of "tomorrow" to be quiet. I would promise myself to stick to anything for 3–4 weeks (not shorter), and if it still did not feel better by then, I would stop doing it. The most challenging part was to stay aware of the habit that I wanted to change, so I did not go on autopilot and revert to my old behavior.

Sometimes it would slip my awareness and I would have to start over again while remaining kind and relaxed.

To stay compassionate with myself, I made an internal agreement. If the tool to change the habit did not work, it was simply not the right fit for me and that I needed to look for another way to make the desired change. This mindset allowed me to mitigate the narrative away from self-talk like *I failed; I am lazy, stupid, unworthy or not good enough* that is the destroyer of progress.

The daily rituals and practices I described in this book are my anchors among the rush that our busy world entails. I have made the unshakable decision to practice every day and therefore do not need to use finite willpower to reconfirm my day-to-day choices. These rituals and practices are now part of my DNA; they are not what I do—they are who I am. This mindset shift is incredibly liberating and grounding.

I also celebrate all the little successes I notice, which build my trust in the process. Today, I am so convinced that mindfulness and meditation work that I no longer need to track it. Instead, I channel my focus on uplifting emotions like gratitude and awe for life, my family, work, friends, and the world. I know that elevating my emotions is the baseline for ultimate fulfillment.

NEXT LEVEL YOU

Next Level You is not somewhere out there in the future. It is the choices that we make moment-to-moment in our lives. It is here and now. Mindfulness is all about the present moment because it is the only moment we get to live in, act on, and experience. Have you ever physically been to the past or the future? I bet not! Everything after this present moment is a fantasy and a construct of the mind.

The egoistic untrained mind makes us feel like life is a constant battle and we need to push, achieve, and work hard at it. The nervous system will weaken because it cannot handle all the complexity, and as a failsafe, the body lets the mind check out, spending time in the future or the past as an escape.

The more present we are, the more creative and fluid our lives become. Just like everything in nature, life starts to unfold in a beautiful flow of events, people, places, and magical synchronicities. It all starts to come effortlessly. This effortlessness is the *Next Level You.*

Are you ready to live in the state of flow to reach the *Next Level You?* The time is now.

ACCESS TO MINDFULNESS TOOLS:

I hope now you feel inspired and energized to add and practice more mindfulness and meditation in your work and life. To access more tools and resources, use code NEXTLEVEL for one month of free access to the Online Mindfulness Platform (www.SattvaMeOnline.com), which contains video recordings of meditations, breathing exercises, webinars, and other fantastic resources and information to start your practice today.

To learn more about the workshops, meditation initiation, and techniques described in this book, please visit
www.Sattva.Me.

To hire Oksana as a speaker, please visit
www.OksanaEsberard.com.

HEAR IT FROM OUR CLIENTS:

I was thrilled to introduce SattvaMe to my organization and bring mindfulness into the workplace. Practicing meditation and breathing techniques with my leadership team before strategic meetings has allowed us to be more focused, present, and unified. No matter what level of mindfulness each individual practice, we collectively agree that we feel more calm, aware, and equipped to tackle a challenge and be creative in developing solutions when starting off with a guided mindfulness exercise from a gifted coach like Oksana.

My meditation and yoga journey began more than 12 years ago, but I am reminded often that it is a journey and a practice, not a destination. You simply have to start, surrender, and enjoy the ride!

KRISTA WADE
*General Manager at New Horizons Computer
Learning Centers of South Florida*

For as long as I can recall, my mind was always racing 100 miles per hour. I could not ever imagine quieting it, let alone getting to a point where I go to sleep virtually every night in a relaxed and reflective state and wake in silence, stillness . . . as opposed to noise and the nonsense of trying to tackle my day before it even begins.

"Peace does not mean to be in a place where there is no chaos, trouble, or hard realities to deal with. Peace means to be in the midst of all of those things and still remain mentally, emotionally, and physically centered."

I forget where I read this quote and who to attribute it to, but I will never forget what it says because it captures the essence of my journey and practice with meditation and mindfulness.

Through my work with Oksana, my life has been demonstrably altered for the better. I'm not sure how I could consciously lead a mindful life with a cluttered and noisy mind. That is the magic of meditation. Oksana has expertly played the role of teacher, mentor, and chief accountability officer to help me start and sustain my daily practice!

In my opinion, my thoughts control just about

everything. So, I am constantly striving to stay acutely aware of how I feel and what is my self-talk every second and minute of each day. Through staying mindful, I am aware of thoughts, feelings, and reactions from a detached perspective.

I believe that meditation and my ability to consistently practice is the necessary foundation for mindful living. I am eternally grateful to Oksana for helping me transform my life in the most meaningfully healthy way I can imagine.

DOUG SKOKE

Business Development Director, Benjamin Douglas Consulting

Training with Oksana has changed my life. I started working with her and embraced the tools of mindfulness and meditation to help me heal after going through a sudden divorce. I was not at all expecting it after being in a 12-year relationship. I was struggling with anxiety and depression. I felt lost and afraid and did not know myself.

I had met Oksana at work, where through SattvaMe she helped my leadership team clear our heads, become more present, and stay focused before our quarterly strategic planning meetings. After seeing the impact she had on our team, I began to work with Oksana on a private basis.

I had no idea how I was going to get through the changes brought by divorce and how I was going to rebuild my life. I felt like I had lost everything. Oksana taught me meditation, breathing exercises and helped me see life and presented challenges in a new light.

Mindfulness practices have completely transformed my life. I now use meditation and breathing techniques Oksana has taught me every day. Her practices have helped me stay focused, energized, and have brought so much joy into my life.

I feel I am able to handle stressful situations in a calm and focused way. I believe the practice has made me so much more self-aware and present. I also feel the practices of mindfulness and meditation have helped me become a better leader. I'm more empathetic and live a life based on gratitude and compassion.

I am now able to control anxiety and have mastered being able to change my mood using the tools and practices Oksana has taught me. Every time we meet, I learn more and more about myself. She has helped me get to a spiritual level I have never experienced before. I feel I have been able to manifest so many beautiful opportunities just by practicing and setting my intentions every morning after the meditation.

I love working with Oksana and I am excited to meet with her every month. I learn so much from every session and get so much out of working with her. She keeps me challenged, motivated, and helps me view all things in the perspective of curiosity. Oksana has changed my life and I am so grateful for the mindfulness practices she has taught me.

STEPHANIE CRUZ

Director of Talent Acquisition at New Horizons Computer Learning Center of South Florida

Because of Oksana, I have meditated daily over the past six months (and counting!). She helped me set my morning ritual of getting up early, meditating, and doing light exercise or having breakfast with my husband.

Because of this new morning ritual, I have felt a material difference in the way I perform at work each day. I feel more flexible when faced with challenges, and I know that when things don't go quite as planned, I can step away and take a mini mental break with meditation and breathing exercises. I have learned a lot on this journey and still have so much more to learn!

KAITLYN ERSEK

Director of Marketing, Holganix LLC

Working with Oksana has been life changing. Her tools and knowledge have taught me how to get naturally high on energy and thrive in life.

One morning while meditating, I found myself making a new facial expression. I had no clue what face I was making, though I knew I had never oriented my mouth and cheeks in this particular way. It felt completely foreign to me. Oksana taught me to embrace whatever comes up during practice, so I rolled with it and found myself in the same facial position for the better part of 15 minutes. After completing my morning practice, I felt a sense of peace and joy that was ideal.

Out of pure curiosity, I placed myself in front of a mirror and attempted to make the face I experienced during my practice.

Reassembling it purely from memory, I was eager to learn what this new expression looked like in the mirror. Within a fraction of a second, the following chain of events occurred. With my eyes closed, first, I positioned my face as I remembered it felt during the meditation. Second, I confirmed that it felt the same way as a few minutes before. When I looked into a mirror, I found myself smiling broader and brighter than I ever have in my entire life.

Moments like this, while surreal, are quite common when working with Oksana and implementing her teachings. I implore you to follow the lessons in this book. You will truly enjoy it.

RYAN MARKEL
Entrepreneur Coach, Petra Coach

ABOUT THE AUTHOR

Oksana Esberard is a certified business Mindfulness + Meditation expert, international speaker, and bestselling author. Utilizing her talent and multicultural background to bridge the ancient 5000-year old wisdom to tangible business results, Oksana supports it by science and modern practicality. She leads corporate mindfulness programs and retreats for entrepreneurs, small businesses and Inc. 500 companies around the world.

Oksana has trained extensively in the Indian Himalayas at the top meditation school, Sattva Yoga Academy, where she continues to evolve her practice and knowledge. She has completed a Mindfulness-Based Stress Reduction Program in the U.S. as well as a Transcendental Meditation program in Hong Kong. She continuously evolves her expertise through advanced training and retreats by Anand Mehrotra, Dr.

Joe Dispenza, Tony Robbins, Tommy Rosen, Gurmukh Khalsa, Kia Miller, and other renown masters.

As the newest addition, Oksana works with maximum security prisons bringing meditation and mindfulness as tools of self-correction for those who want a second chance in life.

When not traveling or hosting Mindfulness + Meditation events, Oksana enjoys biking to the beach to meet the sunrise and playing with her dog Lola.

Born and raised in the Far East of Russia, Oksana became a citizen of the world at the age of 16. She has traveled to 55+ countries, leading executive events and workshops in India, North America, and Russia.

REFERENCES

"Autoimmune Disease Statistics." AARDA (website). American Autoimmune Related Diseases Association Inc. www.aarda.org/news-information/statistics/#1488234345468-3bf2d325-1052.

Bradberry, Travis. "13 Things Ridiculously Successful People Do Every Day." LinkedIn. www.linkedin.com/pulse/13-things-ridiculously-successful-people-do-every-day-bradberry/. March 26, 2019.

Csikszentmihalyi, Mihaly. *Flow and the Foundations of Positive* Psychology: The Collected Works of Mihaly Csikszentmihalyi. Dordrecht: Springer, 2014.

Currin, Andrew. "U Drive. U Text. U Pay." NHTSA (website). United States Department of Transportation. www.nhtsa.gov/risky-driving/distracted-driving. May 8, 2019.

"Deaths of Despair: The Opioid Epidemic Is Just Part of the Problem." ScienceDaily (website). ScienceDaily. www.sciencedaily.com/releases/2018/09/180927164235.html. September 27, 2018.

"Delaying Gratification." APA.org. American Psychological Association. www.apa.org/helpcenter/willpower-gratification.pdf.

Deutschman, Alan. "Change or Die." Fast Company. May 1, 2005. Available at www.fastcompany.com/52717/change-or-die.

Ferriss, Timothy. *Tools of Titans: The Tactics, Routines, and Habits of Billionaires, Icons, and World-Class Performers.* New York: Houghton Mifflin Harcourt, 2017.

Howe, Neil. "America The Sleep-Deprived." Forbes (website). Forbes. www.forbes.com/sites/neilhowe/2017/08/18/america-the-sleep-deprived/#154ef75b1a38. August 8, 2017.

"Hustle 2.0: About." Hustle 2.0 (website). Hustle 2.0. https://www.hustle20.com.

"IBM 2010 Global CEO Study: Creativity Selected as Most Crucial Factor for Future Success." IBM (website). IBM. www-03.ibm.com/press/us/en/pressrelease/31670.wss. May 18, 2010.

Impact Theory Team. "Yuval Noah Harari: The 2 Most Important Skills for the Rest of Your Life." Impact Theory (website). Impact Theory www.impacttheory.com/episode/yuval-noah-harari/. November 13, 2018.

Killingsworth, Matt A. and Daniel T. Gilbert. "A Wandering Mind Is an Unhappy Mind." *Science Magazine*. Vol. 330, Issue 6006, pp 932. doi:10.1126/science.1192439. November 12, 2010.

Lavitt, John. "Dr. Gabor Maté on the Trauma Underlying the Stigma of Addiction: An Interview." The Fix (website). The Fix. www.thefix. com/dr-gabor-mate-trauma-underlying-stigma-addiction-interview. December 12, 2017.

Mindful Staff. "Jon Kabat-Zinn: Defining Mindfulness." Mindful.org. Mindful. www.mindful.org/jon-kabat-zinn-defining-mindfulness/. January 11, 2017.

Nordgren, Loran, Rachel Ruttan, and Mary-Hunter McDonnell. "It's Harder to Empathize with People If You've Been in Their Shoes." Harvard Business Review. *Harvard Business Review.* www.hbr. org/2015/10/its-harder-to-empathize-with-people-if-youve-been-in-their-shoes. October 20, 2015.

Oschman, James L., Gaétan Chevalier and Richard Brown. "The Effects of Grounding (Earthing) on Inflammation, the Immune Response, Wound Healing, and Prevention and Treatment of Chronic Inflammatory and Autoimmune Diseases." Journal of Inflammation Research. Dove Medical Press. www.ncbi.nlm.nih.gov/pmc/articles/PMC4378297/. March 24, 2015.

P&S Market Research. "Chronic Pain Treatment Market to Reach $105.9 Billion by 2024: P&S Intelligence." P&S Intelligence. Available at www.globenewswire.com/news-release/2019/01/07/1680944/0/en/Chronic-Pain-Treatment-Market-to-Reach-105-9-Billion-by-2024-P-S-Intelligence.html. January 7, 2019.

"Shakti Healing Circle: Awakening the Power Within." Shakti Healing Circle (website). Shakti Healing Circle. www.shaktihealingcircle.com/.

Singer, Michael. *The Surrender Experiment: My Journey into Life's Perfection.* New York: Harmony Books, 2015.

Tiffander, NJ, et al. "Effect of Sleep Deprivation on Surgeons' Dexterity on Laparoscopy Simulator." The Lancet. The Lancet. www.thelancet.com/journals/lancet/article/PIIS0140-6736(98)00034-8/fulltext. October 10, 1998.

www.ingramcontent.com/pod-product-compliance
Lightning Source LLC
Chambersburg PA
CBHW072135020426
42334CB00018B/1816